Chris C. Pinney, DVM

German Shorthaired Pointers

Everything About Purchase, Care, Nutrition, Behavior, and Training

Filled with Full-color Photographs

BARRON'S

CONTENTS

THE GERMAN SHORTHAIRED POINTER: A BRIEF HISTORY

To trace the history and ancestry of this remarkable breed, one must travel back through history to nineteenth-century Europe.

The rise of the German Empire under Prussian leadership was in full swing during the mid-1800s. For the first time, the army, which up to this time had been made up chiefly of the Prussian aristocracy and peasantry, was opened up to the middle class. This, combined with sweeping economic and political changes occurring throughout Europe, led to a rise in the status of the middle class within the Empire.

With this rise came increased privileges regarding land ownership and hunting. In previous centuries, it was usually only the kings, princes, and nobles who had the right to hunt, and they owned vast tracks of land for this pur-

Highly intelligent, with an incredibly strong desire to please their owners, GSPs are also famous for their gentle dispositions and affectionate natures.

pose. However, as the wealth of middle-class Prussia grew during the 1800s, merchants, professionals, and other middle-class citizens were able to purchase or lease land for themselves on which, of course, they could hunt.

Fulfilling a Need

In Germany dense forests blended with open fields and housed all types of feather and fur, including grouse, rabbit, fox, deer, wolves, and wild boar. It was there that the Teutonic hunters wanted to create a breed of hunting dog that could effectively hunt all types of game in all types of terrain that their country had to offer. They wanted a dog with a nose sensitive enough to locate game at an acceptable, useful distance. Because German hunters typically hunted on foot, they also wanted a dog that had enough discipline and inbred instinct to remain staunch on point once the game was located to allow hunters time to close in on the quarry. A hunting partner was needed that would retrieve fallen game for them both on land and in water. In addition, the dog needed to be bold and aggressive enough to interact with and track larger game such as wild cats, foxes, and deer within the deep German forests. Finally, and very importantly, these hunters wanted a household companion that could be relied upon to protect the home and those in it effectively when called upon to do so. Keeping all of these qualities in mind, the seed of this dream was effectively planted, and the work was begun to develop such a dog.

Origins and Ancestry

Many different theories exist regarding the actual origins and ancestry of the German Shorthaired Pointer (GSP), but most experts believe that the breed development was initiated by a cross between the old Spanish pointer and traditional continental pointers, including the German Pointer and Braque Français (Table 1). German hunters decided to further cross the breed with tracking hounds such as the German Bloodhound and French Gascon to further enhance scenting ability and to soften the temperament of the emerging breed. The genes of these German tracking hounds also helped to overcome many of the unwanted or undesirable characteristics of the traditional pointers, including reduced trailing ability, a natural aversion for water work, and a noted lack of aggressiveness toward predators.

Even with all these improvements, early breeders were still not satisfied. The dogs that were created from the previous crosses were proving

Table 1: Breeds Believed to Have Played a Role in the Development of the German Shorthaired Pointer

- Old Spanish Pointer
- German Bloodhound
- English Pointer
- English Foxhound
- Old German Pointer
- French Gascon
- French Braque

to be too slow in the hunt and lacking in true agility. In addition, these hunters liked the scenting prowess that came from the bloodhound, yet didn't want their new breed to look like a bloodhound. As a result, during the 1860's, still another cross was made with the English pointer to improve the speed, style, looks, and pointing instincts of the breed. The end product of all of these efforts was a sleek, good-looking, intelligent, loyal, and versatile gundog with incredible stamina, an acute sense of smell, a highly developed pointing instinct, and an eagerness to retrieve fallen game either on land or in water. Now the German hunter had a companion that could trail and scent both furred and feathered game, could point and retrieve game birds, and had the size, strength, and courage to interact with larger game such as deer, fox, and boar. These dogs were real performers.

The German Shorthaired Pointer in Europe

In 1872 the first GSP made its way into the German Kennel Club Stud Book. His name: Hektor I ZK I. Eleven years later, two GSPs named Nero and Treff competed against each other in the German Derby of 1883. As it turned out, both would end up becoming great foundation dogs for the breed (Nero's daughter Flora would later produce three offspring named Walden, Waldo, and Hertha, all of which can be credited with laying the foundation of many of the great pedigree lines we see today.)

The popularity of the new breed soon spread across the European continent. England was slow to accept the breed's popularity, owing to the fact that much of the hunting done in that island nation was accomplished on horseback and in open fields. This type of hunting required a dog with a much broader range and speed than the GSP could provide. In addition, national pride in the English pointing breeds undoubtedly contributed to this slow acceptance of the GSP.

In 1887 the GSP did appear on exhibit in England at the Barns Elms Show. However, its introduction was short-lived, and GSPs were not seen with regularity in Britain until after World War II. The breed's popularity continued to flourish on the Continent, and in 1891 the Klub Kurzhaar was founded for the purpose of maintaining the standards and guidelines for this new and exciting type of sporting dog.

The German Shorthaired Pointer in America

In 1925 Dr. Charles Thorton of Missoula, Montana, a physician and staunch upland game hunter, introduced an Austrian female GSP named Senta von Hohenbruch into the United States. At the time, she came from the top of the German-Austrian bloodline of GSPs, as did many of those that followed. Although it is probable that a number of GSPs entered America with German immigrant masters prior to 1925, Dr. Thorton is rightly given credit as being the "father" of the breed in the United States and was instrumental in increasing awareness of the breed across America.

Initially, skepticism concerning the breed's abilities slowed the growth of this popularity. However, the GSP soon proved itself as a formidable hunter and became a very popular dog with American hunters, who, like their German counterparts, enjoyed hunting on foot.

AKC Recognition

In 1930, the breed was recognized by the American Kennel Club, with Grief v.d. Fliegerhalde becoming the first GSP registered with the organization. The first national AKC (American Kennel Club) licensed specialty show was held in 1941 at the International Kennel Club show in Chicago, Illinois. Field trials soon emerged in 1944, the first being an AKC-licensed event held in Minnesota by the German Shorthaired Pointer Club of America. This club today is the AKC Parent Club and official sponsor of the breed in the United States. Promoting the GSP's popularity as a versatile hunter, the German Shorthaired Pointer Club of America has built a solid foundation for the breed and its development for years to come. Today the GSP falls within the top 20 of all breeds registered by the AKC.

A Prussian officer with his Shorthair companions.

OWNING A GERMAN SHORTHAIRED POINTER

Although GSPs were originally developed for hunting, years of domestication have produced an outstanding house pet.

Highly affectionate and loving dogs, GSPs quickly form close bonds with their owners. As house dogs, they are relatively clean and easy to maintain. Smart and readily trainable, GSPs can quickly adjust to almost any living environment. However, prior to making the commitment to purchase a GSP, there are several questions you need to ask yourself and, in turn, feel very comfortable with your answers:

✔ Why do I want a GSP in the first place?
✔ Do I want a puppy or do I want a more mature dog?
✔ Do I want a male or a female?
✔ Do I want a trained or untrained GSP?
✔ How will my children (if applicable) be affected by my new GSP?
✔ Do I have other pets in the household that will be affected by this new addition?

Ask yourself: Why do you want a GSP in the first place?

✔ Am I willing to house my GSP indoors?
✔ Am I willing to accept the financial and time responsibilities associated with GSP ownership?

By addressing these issues ahead of time, you can spare yourself from unexpected surprises and regrets, knowing that you have indeed made the correct decision prior to bringing your new friend home.

Why Do I Want a GSP?

The GSP is a fun-loving breed that is capable of exhibiting lots of affection, loyalty, and spunk. These dogs are perfectly capable of fulfilling many roles as pets—you must recognize which role(s) you expect yours to play.

Companion: As a companion, it is hard to find one as much fun and as satisfying as the GSP. Highly intelligent, with an incredibly strong desire to please their owners, GSPs are

known for their gentle dispositions and affectionate natures. These qualities make them excellent choices for households with children.

Protectors: Although they have gentle and easygoing natures, rest assured that these dogs can become formidable protectors if they feel any members of their pack are threatened. Possessing keen senses, especially the sense of smell, they are able to detect the presence of danger long before their owners.

Exercise: By nature, this is a very energetic and active breed, and as such, GSPs need to be able to expend lots of calories throughout the day. They make great exercise partners—that is, if you can keep up the pace! Because of their size, they may not do particularly well in apartment or townhouse settings, or in small kennel enclosures, in which an area to run may be limited. They need space: Space to run, space to play, and space to unleash their instinctive desires for the hunt.

Bonding: GSPs are especially responsive to the authority of their trainers or owners, which in itself has a highly positive influence on the bonding that occurs between owner and dog, and upon the training process. Rarely do they get their feelings hurt when reprimanded. When they do, they seem to bounce back and recapture their positive attitudes quite rapidly.

Trainability: Trainability, along with the GSP's intelligence, looks, and strong will, make it a formidable competitor. Owners wishing to compete in AKC- or FDSB (Field Dog Stud Book)-sanctioned events with their GSPs will not be disappointed. Nor will they be disappointed if they want to use their GSPs for hunting. These dogs are by far the most popular general utility gundogs found in North America today, able to locate, point, and retrieve game with excellent efficiency.

Puppy or Adult?

The decision on whether to purchase a puppy or adult dog is again strictly your preference. There are many adult GSPs that are surrendered to shelters and pounds simply because their owners could not care for them properly. These dogs are just begging for a good, loving home. The advantage, of course, of choosing a more mature GSP is that you miss the trials and tribulations associated with puppyhood, including chewing, biting, and house-training. Many adult GSPs are fully trained when you get them, which saves a tremendous amount of time and effort. Also, an adult dog that has been properly cared for has usually had all of its initial series of immunizations, saving you the costs associated with the initial series of puppy checkups and shots.

Obviously, the disadvantage of choosing an adult dog is that training (including house-training) may never have occurred or worse yet, the GSP may never have been properly socialized to other pets and/or people. Also, a personality or health defect may have prompted the previous owner to relinquish the dog. As a result, be sure to obtain as much information as you can regarding the dog's past and request an in-home test period prior to making a full-fledged commitment to adopt such a dog.

The advantage of purchasing a puppy instead of an adult is that you have a chance to form a stronger, more emotional bond with your dog. Puppies between the ages of eight and twelve weeks of age are in their peak period of socialization and readily form these bonds. They are also quite responsive to any training they are given during this time.

Male or Female?

Deciding upon the sex of your new GSP is strictly a matter of preference. Both male and female GSPs make excellent pets. Male dogs tend to be more spirited and protective, whereas females are generally regarded as more affectionate and trainable. However, such qualities will vary between individual dogs, and will be influenced by factors such as genetics, training, and neutering.

Trained or Untrained?

This decision will be influenced by the time you will have available to devote to training, the confidence you have in your ability to do the training, the extent of actual training and refinement you desire for your dog, and the amount of money you are willing to spend on the process.

Purchasing an untrained puppy affords you the opportunity to closely bond with it during its peak socialization period, which occurs between eight and twelve weeks of age. In addition, you will be able to experience the satisfaction of transforming an inexperienced puppy into a trained companion. Still another advantage of purchasing an untrained puppy is cost, as its price tag is considerably less than that of a partially or fully trained GSP. The disadvantage of purchasing an untrained puppy comes in the time required to mold it into an obedient friend. You also run the risk of training mistakes, many of which might be avoided with prior professional training.

Professional Trainers: Some owners opt to purchase an untrained puppy and then hire

professional trainers to work their magic. This option is fine as long as you plan to be with your puppy at every training session. Shipping your puppy off to a remote location to be trained by a stranger after it has just settled into a new home with you is not a good idea. Such an action would put incredible emotional stress on your friend and could lead to behavioral problems in the future.

Purchasing a trained dog provides immediate gratification and saves time. The risk of training mistakes is greatly minimized and the chances of obtaining a dog with serious behavioral or physical problems are virtually eliminated. As mentioned earlier, the biggest disadvantage of purchasing a trained dog is its price. Fully trained GSPs can cost three to four times as

much as untrained pups, depending upon the level of instruction received.

Your GSP and Children

Before bringing an adult GSP home where there are children, you must be certain that the dog has been properly socialized to children. The best way to do this is to take your children with you to visit and interact with the pet at the seller's location. If the dog shows any degree of aggressiveness or shyness around your children, look for another selection. The big advantage of purchasing a puppy less than 16 weeks of age is the opportunity gained to socialize it specifically to your children. However, remember that negative socialization can also occur if a puppy is abused or mishandled in any way by a child, often resulting in aggressiveness toward that child when the puppy matures.

Your GSP and Existing Pets

Anticipate any jealousies or incompatibilities that a new GSP in the home would create among your existing pets. A most important consideration is how well your other pets have been socialized to dogs and whether or not your new GSP himself has been socialized to other dogs and cats. If you have a pet at home that already attacks and/or runs from anything that moves on four legs, you could have a serious behavioral challenge on your hands when you bring home a new dog. Also, an unsocialized dog will often fight any new dog that trespasses into its territory. If you have pocket pets at home, such as guinea pigs, rabbits, and ferrets, keep in mind what GSPs were originally bred for and make sure that all interactions between your GSP and these pets are supervised.

Time and Money

Basic Expenses

With GSP ownership comes many responsibilities in terms of finances and time. Financial responsibilities include those costs associated with basic items such as dog bowls, training devices, and food, not to mention healthcare (see Table 4). Extracurricular activities, such as competitive events, specialized training, and hunting excursions will also add to yearly expenditures. If you travel a lot with your job or your family, boarding fees can accumulate rapidly, and you will need to plan on budgeting for such expenses as well.

Table 2: Factors to Consider Prior to Purchasing a German Shorthaired Pointer

- Age (Puppy; Young Adult; Adult)
- Sex (Male versus Female; Neutered versus Intact)
- Source (Local breeder; Out-of-town; Mail Order)
- Expenses Associated with Ownership (Food; Veterinary; Training; Competitions)
- Prior Training (None; Started; Fully Trained)
- Housing (Indoors versus Outdoors)

Medical Insurance

Be prepared to set aside money for your pet's medical insurance. Certainly there may be unexpected illnesses or injuries that could catch you off guard financially and cause you to make decisions that you may not want to make, but are forced to because of money. If you don't want to purchase an insurance policy for your pet (and many are available on the market today), consider self-insuring your GSP by setting up monthly contributions into a special "pet" fund.

Quality Time

Be sure to schedule quality time with your GSP every day just as you would any other appointment or activity. This interaction can be in the form of exercise, play, or training. It should also include a few minutes of simply petting and talking to your dog. Daily brushing sessions will also benefit your dog not only emotionally but physically as well. After all, who doesn't like to have their backs scratched or rubbed on occasion! Take full advantage of the greatest benefit of owning a dog—the human-companion animal bond. It has been proven that this bond harbors therapeutic health benefits for both parties.

Considering it is not unusual for GSPs to live well over 12 years when properly cared for, the decision to bring a new dog into the home carries with it long-term responsibility. As a result, always think before you act and reflect upon these responsibilities prior to going shopping.

FINDING YOUR GERMAN SHORTHAIRED POINTER

So where do you begin your search for your GSP? A good place to start is your local or national breed association; it should be able to direct you to a number of reputable breeders and/or trainers in your area.

Where to Start

If your pointer is simply going to be a house pet, why not contact your local GSP rescue group and adopt a foster dog in search of a permanent home? Perform a web search or contact the AKC to obtain the phone number of your local organization.

If you're looking for a hunter, hunting clubs and shooting preserves can provide a wealth of information. In addition, most sporting journals, hunting magazines, and dog-related publications are full of advertisements for trained and untrained gun dogs, as well as potential show dogs. Prices can vary depending upon pedigrees and levels of training.

Pedigree

Before you pay a lot of money for your dog, request a copy of the dog's pedigree back at

A GSP is a loyal and trusting friend.

least five generations. It would certainly be helpful if this pedigree was full of ancestral champions in conformation, companion, and performance events, as indicated by the abbreviations listed next to the names on the list. Of course, no inbreeding (having common ancestors in the first or second generations) should be evident within the pedigree.

Visit the Breeder

If feasible, visit the breeder on location. If the premises are filthy and poorly maintained, don't stick around. Leave. If the premises are acceptable, ask to see the parents of your potential selection. Both should be in excellent health, free of physical defects, and possess an impressive conformation and pleasing personality. Request a copy of their health records to be sure neither has been diagnosed with a genetic disease common to the breed (see Table 3). Also, don't forget to perform a physical

Table 3: Genetic Predispositions to Disease in German Shorthaired Pointers

Condition	System/Area Affected	Clinical Signs
Acute Moist Dermatitis	Skin	Moist bacterial skin infection
Amaurotic idiocy	Nervous system	Weakness; seizures; abnormal behavior
Cataracts	Eyes	Cloudiness of eyes; blindness
Diabetes Insipidus	Kidneys	Increased water consumption; increased urination
Entropion	Eyes	Chronic eye discharge/infection; usually both eyes
Eversion of the Nictitating Membrane	Eyes	Eye redness/discharge
Gastric Dilatation/Volvulus	Stomach	Bloated abdomen; vomiting; weakness
Hemivertebrae	Spinal column	Hindlimb weakness/paralysis; incontinence
Hip Dysplasia	Hip joints	Hindlimb lameness
Hypothyroidism	Multiple systems	Obesity; lethargy; skin, and neurologic disorders
Lupoid Dermatosis	Skin	Scales and crusts on face, ears, and back
Lymphedema	Limbs	Swelling of limbs due to poor lymph drainage
Nasal Carcinoma	Nose	Tumor involving nose
Oropharyngeal Neoplasia	Mouth	Tumor involving tissues of mouth
Pannus	Eyes	Cloudy or pigmented corneas; blindness
Progressive Retinal Atrophy	Eyes	Blindness
Pseudohermaphroditism	Reproductive	Abnormal testicle development
Subaortic Stenosis	Heart	Weakness; breathing difficulty; abdominal swelling
Von Willebrand's Disease	Blood	Poor blood clotting; blood in urine/feces; nosebleeding

exam (see Physical Exam Checklist, page 40) on one or both parents.

Physical Exam

Perform this same physical exam on the individual you're thinking of buying. Assess its personality. Pick up the puppy and cradle him in your arms. Does he struggle or fuss when you do? If so, move on to the next selection. The puppy you want should not be shy and hesitant to interact with you, yet he also should not be too overbearing and rambunctious. Your final selection should have a personality that falls somewhere between these two extremes.

Trial Period

If it is not possible to pick out your dog in person, request a 30-day trial period prior to

Prior to purchase, request a copy of your dog's pedigree.

the payment of any money, during which you can test your dog's personality and temperament. Most reputable breeders and trainers stand behind the quality of their dogs and rarely have a problem with such arrangements. If the dog proves to be unsatisfactory for any reason, most will allow you to return it with no questions asked.

Competitive Events

If you are planning on entering your GSP in competitive events, find a dog with a championship pedigree. Of course, such a selection will come with a higher price tag, but if you are serious about competing, it will no doubt give

you and your dog the edge needed to win in the show ring.

Registration Application

Upon purchase, the breeder will give you an AKC registration application, which has been partially filled-out with information pertaining to your dog's characteristics, pedigree, and date of birth. Finish filling out this form with your name, address, and the name you would like your dog registered under, and mail it and the application fee directly to the American Kennel Club. The AKC will then send you an official registration certificate for safekeeping.

BRINGING HOME YOUR NEW DOG

Prior to bringing home your new dog, you'll want to do everything in your power to make him feel comfortable and secure in his surroundings. Some minor planning on your part can make the transition much easier for him.

Table 4 contains a handy checklist of items you should purchase prior to your dog's arrival. Also, decide ahead of time which family member is going to be responsible for feeding, training, and grooming the dog. After all, if it doesn't get assigned, you'll end up having to do it all.

Housing Considerations

Dogs, including GSPs, should be housed indoors, not outdoors. Why? Dogs are pack animals and those housed indoors (with their pack members) are more emotionally stable than those kept outdoors, isolated from their owners. As a result, dogs housed outdoors can

Ownership means investment in terms of both time and money.

develop a wide variety of behavioral issues not commonly seen in those individuals kept indoors, such as digging, nuisance barking, and other forms of destructive and irritating behavior.

Preparing Your Home

Before you arrive home with your new dog, prepare a special area or room that it can claim as its den and sleeping quarters. When you initially get a puppy home, this is the first place to which it should be introduced. Make the experience a pleasurable one. Praise your puppy enthusiastically and offer it a food treat in order to associate that location with pleasure. If bringing a mature dog home, ask the breeder beforehand where the dog slept while at the breeder's house and, if possible, allow the dog access to a similar location within your home.

Dog-proofing Indoors

When keeping a dog (and especially a puppy) indoors, there are a number of safety measures you should implement within your house to "dog-proof" it.

✔ Put all plants out of reach. Puppies love to chew on plants, and could harm themselves if they ingest a poisonous variety.

✔ Keep all electrical cords well out of reach. This may mean banishing your playful pet from certain areas of the house, but this is a minor inconvenience compared to a potentially fatal accident. Again, puppies love to chew, and electrical cords are mighty appetizing to unrefined tastes.

✔ Keep everything that's not a toy picked up, including spare change. Pennies and other coins can cause severe gastroenteritis or obstructions if swallowed. Puppies naturally explore their environments with their mouths, and will pick up (and often eat) just about anything.

✔ Confine your GSP to non-carpeted floors until it's properly housetrained (see HOW-TO, page 26). Even so-called "stain resistant" carpets may not uphold this claim after repeated bombardments.

Table 4: Equipment and Accessories for Your New GSP

✔ Crate/travel kennel
✔ Food and water bowls
✔ Training aids (see Table 12, page 64)
✔ Odor neutralizer
✔ Name tag for collar
✔ Toys/chew bones
✔ Food
✔ Grooming accessories
  • Bristle brush
  • Nail trimmers
  • Toothbrush
  • Toothpaste
  • Ear cleanser
✔ Heartworm preventive medication
✔ Flea control products
✔ First aid kit

Naming Your New Dog

Naming your new addition should be fun and involve the entire family. You can even find entire books devoted to choosing the right name for your dog at your favorite bookstore. Stick to names having two syllables. This will allow your dog to easily differentiate between his name and those one-syllable commands that he will learn during obedience and field training. You can further set his name apart by adding a vowel sound to the end of it. Be con-

sistent when using the name. If you name your dog "Nifta," don't shorten it on occasion to "Nif." You'll only confuse your pet as to his true identity.

First Encounters

When you bring home a new puppy, its first encounters with your family members are important. Initial introductions, whether with children or other adults in the family, are always positive.

✔ Supervise children-pet interactions carefully, and stress to the former the importance of gentle play and handling.

✔ Instruct your children on the proper way to pick up and hold the new puppy. Dogs should not be picked up solely by the front legs or by the neck; instead, the entire body should be lifted as one unit with both the front end and hind end supported.

Playing and Chewing

After periods of play, your puppy needs time to rest. It is fine to play hard with your puppy, but overt roughhousing should be avoided. If a play session progresses from a friendly romp to an all-out frontal assault, end it immediately. Your puppy needs to learn how to control his activity level to an intensity that is socially acceptable.

The same applies to chewing. It's perfectly natural for a puppy to want to explore his environment and express himself with his mouth. During play there will be times when he will bite and nip; when this occurs, simply and strongly say "*No*," and provide a chew toy as a substitute. If you plan to train a hunter, avoid playing any type of "tug-of-war" with your puppy; doing so creates a dog with a "hard mouth" when it comes to retrieving birds.

Toys

Toys that you purchase for your new GSP to play with should be made of nylon, rawhide, or hard rubber. Of the three, the first is most desirable because it is most easily digestible if swallowed. Rawhides are fine if the dog takes his time and doesn't swallow them whole. For those that won't, avoid rawhides altogether, as big pieces can cause serious stomach upset and sometimes intestinal blockages if swallowed. Also, some dogs have difficulty differentiating rawhide from leather, which could put your new pair of shoes in serious jeopardy. Rubber chew toys should be solid, as to not be easily ripped apart by sharp puppy teeth. Avoid chew toys with plastic "squeaks." These can be easily extracted by most dogs, and can be swallowed or aspirated into

═══ TIP ═══

Toys

Don't use old socks, shoes, or sweatshirts as substitute toys for your GSP, because he can't tell the difference between old and new. Allow a puppy to chew on an old shoe while still an adolescent and you may find him fancying your expensive leather shoes as an adult.

airways. Regardless of the type of chew toy you pick, choose it as you would a toy for a child. If its design seems flawed, put it back and choose a safer one.

Your attempts to house-train your puppy should start as early as eight weeks of age. This is the beginning of your puppy's period of stable learning. However, before starting, make certain your puppy has been vaccinated and is free of intestinal parasites. The latter is very important because the presence of worms in the intestinal tract will cause unpredictable urges to eliminate.

Use Outdoors for Elimination

For best results, train your dog to use the bathroom outdoors instead of on paper. Owners can't always under-stand why their new puppy has no problems going on newspaper, but just can't get the knack of going outside, when the newspapers aren't there. They seem to forget that, to a puppy, newspaper and grass are two different surfaces with different smells. To first paper-train a puppy, and then expect it to switch over to another type of surface is asking a lot. Also, puppies need to be taught right from the start that the home is "no place to go." By allowing them to eliminate on papers within the house, you are sending them a conflicting message.

Times to Eliminate

Puppies have four fairly predictable times they like to eliminate. These include those periods right after they wake up, right after they eat, right after they exercise or play, and just before they retire at night. Make a concerted effort to take your puppy outside at these times and, if possible, every three to four hours in between.

When you suspect that your puppy has to go to the bathroom (he may start sniffing the ground, circling, and/or look anxious), take him to a defined section of yard far away from the house. (Not only will this make cleanup a snap, it may spare a shoe or prized shrub from an unexpected encounter with a "pile" or urine deposit in a high traffic area within your yard.) If your puppy eliminates, lay on the praise and offer a food treat, then take him back inside immediately. By doing so, he will begin to associate the act of eliminating with the location.

Accidents

If three minutes pass and your puppy hasn't gone, take him back inside anyway. Don't leave him outside to play or

roam. However, watch him closely as he may suddenly change his mind and decide to go.

If it looks like an accident is about to happen, immediately rush your puppy back outside, and follow the same procedure as above. If you happen to catch your puppy in mid-act, simply pick him up and take him outside. Sure, he may finish what he started before you get to the grass, but don't get upset. Place your puppy down on the grass anyway, heap lots of praise on him, then pick him back up and bring him right back inside. Puppies trained in this manner soon realize that their primary business for being outside is to eliminate, not to play.

If accidents happen while training your puppy, don't get upset. That will serve no useful purpose. Simply try to be more attentive next time. Always stick with praise when house-training your puppy. Punishment will serve no purpose except to make your training more difficult, and to possibly desocialize your puppy at the same time.

Note: Whatever you do, don't stick your puppy's nose or face in the excrement in an attempt to prove a point. For some reason, this type of punishment is still quite popular among pet owners, even though it serves no useful purpose. In fact, if you really want to adversely affect your puppy's mental development, that type of behavior is a great way to do it.

Daily Schedules: Establishing a regular feeding and play schedule for your new puppy will make your training easier. Feed no more than twice daily, and take him outside after he finishes each meal. It is preferable to feed the evening portion before 6:00 P.M. This will help reduce the number of overnight accidents that may otherwise occur.

Confinement: To help prevent accidents, keep your puppy in his crate or kennel, or at least in

a confined area at night. This area should be puppy-proofed, and have a floor that won't be damaged if a slip-up occurs. Utility rooms and half-bathrooms work well for this purpose. If an accident occurs during the night or while you are away, don't get upset; as your training sessions progress, you'll find that this will become less and less of a problem. A natural instinct of any canine is to keep its "den" clean. Such inherent instincts, combined with correct house-training efforts on your part, will help fuel the success of your training effort.

Finally, if your puppy does have an accident, use a pet odor neutralizing spray or cleaner instead of a deodorizer on the area in question. These are available at most pet stores, and will in most cases effectively eliminate any lingering scents that may lure your pet back to the same spot.

FEEDING YOUR GERMAN SHORTHAIRED POINTER

There can be little doubt that proper nutrition is the cornerstone of an active, healthy life for your GSP. In addition, good nutritional management can have a profound positive impact on field performance. Fortunately, as the amount of research that supports the link between diet and health increases with each passing day, so do the quality and choice of foods that are available for your pal to eat.

Hundreds of years ago, the diet of most domesticated dogs consisted primarily of table scraps, supplemented by whatever other consumables or prey they could uncover while roaming freely within the confines of their man-made territories. Today, the commercial dog food industry exceeds $100 million per year in the United States alone, with literally hundreds of products and brand names available for the choosing. As a result, your mission as a prudent dog owner is to choose that ration for your GSP that is most nutritionally complete and balanced for his particular stage of life and activity level. Many breeders and trainers advocate the formulation of rations at home using meat and other natural ingredients as raw materials. Although such rations can

Good nutrition equals good health.

provide excellent nutrition, it is vital that they be prepared properly and that they contain a balance of nutrients readily utilizable by the dog. Dog food companies invest millions of dollars in research into their premium foods, ensuring that they are of superior nutritional quality. The bottom line: Unless you simply enjoy putting in the time and effort preparing your GSP's meal, feeding a home-made ration affords no advantages over feeding a high-quality, premium commercial diet.

Nutritional Guidelines for Puppies

Puppyhood begins at birth and lasts for approximately 14 months. During this stage of life, your puppy will need to take in appropriate levels of calcium and phosphorus, protein,

daily allowance into two feedings, the first to be offered in the morning and the second in the evening. Leave the food down for 20 minutes, allowing your puppy to eat all he wishes in that time, and then remove the food entirely until the next meal. Your puppy will quickly learn to eat on schedule.

Table Scraps

Avoid giving table food and scraps to your puppy, as these will surely upset the balance of his daily nutrition. As you know, puppies (especially hungry ones) love to chew. As a result, keep plenty of nylon bones lying about for your pup to chew on between meals.

Water

Fresh water should be accessible at all times. Filtered water is best. Change the water daily and thoroughly clean the water bowl at least once per week.

vitamins, and energy (calories) to ensure proper growth. To make sure that your puppy receives the nutrition he needs for correct development, he should be fed a high-quality, nutritionally balanced premium puppy food. Shop for quality and not price when selecting a food for your puppy. Because there are so many foods out there, ask your veterinarian for a recommendation. Remember that the first year of your puppy's life sets the stage for health and happiness in later years. As a result, to invest in good nutrition during this crucial stage of life is vital.

When feeding high-quality premium diets to your puppy, vitamin and mineral supplementation is generally not required. Feed the manufacturer's recommended daily amount for the size and weight of your little one. Divide the

Nutritional Guidelines for Mature Dogs

At 12 months of age, switch your dog to a maintenance diet for adults. If possible, use the same brand of food (same manufacturer) to ensure that the transition to the adult ration is smooth. Be aware that so-called maintenance foods that make the claim "complete and balanced for all life stages" are actually puppy foods and could lead to obesity and organ stress in adults.

Most adult dogs can be fed just once a day. As far as amounts are concerned, follow the manufacturer's recommended daily feeding amounts, then make some adjustments according to your dog's individual needs and activity levels. For instance, daily caloric needs will generally need to be increased 35 to 40 percent during field training and during hunting season as compared to other times of the year. Also, some dogs will gain weight as they grow older despite eating recommended daily amounts of adult maintenance diets. Reducing the portion size for such a pet may result in an unhappy, hungry dog that whines, begs, and raids the garbage. Instead, if you find that your GSP has put on a few extra pounds along his midsection, he should be placed on a medically supervised weight loss program, consisting of increased exercise and a special diet designed to satisfy hunger pangs while reducing calories.

Treats

Food treats for your GSP are best reserved for training purposes. Feel free, however, to periodically offer your dog fresh vegetables cut into bite-size pieces; these make excellent, low-calorie treats. You'll be surprised how many dogs love to munch on these. The good news is that dogs don't require dietary variations to satisfy psychological cravings. However, once exposed to sweets or high-fat snacks, they can develop cravings that can be difficult to quench.

Bones

Do not offer bones of any kind to your GSP, as they can shatter, splinter, or become lodged in the mouth, throat, and gastrointestinal tract. Bones can also lead to nutritional imbalances by adding unwanted amounts of minerals to the diet. Even rawhide bones can pose a threat to an overzealous pointer that doesn't like to chew his food, as large pieces of slowly digested rawhide can cause gastrointestinal upset, and in severe instances, intestinal block-

---

TIP

Amount of Feeding

During hunting season, feed your dog twice a day, providing 25 percent of the ration two hours prior to the hunt, and the remainder of the diet one hour afterward. Never feed your dog within one hour of rigorous physical activity, as doing so could predispose him to stomach bloat, a dangerous medical condition.

Once hunting season is over, switch back to a regular, lower-calorie maintenance diet. Remember: If activity level does not justify added caloric intake, undesirable weight gain will result.

---

ages. Instead, stick with flavored nylon chew bones, which are easy to digest. These are available at any pet store.

Water

Fresh water (preferably filtered) should be made available at all times for your adult dog. Change the water daily and thoroughly clean the water bowl at least once per week.

Nutritional Guidelines for Senior Adults

Once your GSP reaches seven years of age, dietary changes are warranted to accommodate the effects of aging and the wear and tear on the organ systems of his body. The goal of a senior nutrition program is to provide the highest level of nutrition possible while maintaining

Table 5: Assessing Body Condition

Body Appearance	Ribs	As Seen from the Top	As Seen from the Sides
Too Thin	Ribs easily seen and felt	Marked hourglass figure	Marked abdominal tuck behind ribs
Ideal	Ribs not visible, yet easily felt under thin cover of fat	Mild hourglass figure	Mild abdominal tuck behind ribs
Overweight	Ribs can barely be felt under layer of fat	Waist barely visible or absent	Tuck is barely visible or absent; abdomen distended

ideal body weight, slowing the progression of disease and age-related changes, and reducing or eliminating the clinical manifestations of specific disease conditions. For instance, as your dog's metabolic rate slows and the tendency toward obesity is stronger with advancing age, increasing the amount of fiber and reducing the amount of fat and calories in the diet make sense. As aging kidneys begin to lose their ability to handle the waste materials that must be removed from the body, dietary adjustments can help reduce the amounts of waste products the kidneys have to process. Simply reducing the sodium content of a ration can decrease the workload placed on an aging heart.

Finicky Eaters

Finally, because older pets tend to have reduced sensory output (taste and smell), increasing the palatability of a diet can keep even the most finicky senior satisfied. This can be accomplished by warming the food prior to feeding, mixing a small amount of warm water in with the dry ration, or by adding flavor enhancers recommended by your veterinarian. Older dogs with periodontal disease may lose their appetites due to dental pain. Also, an older dog with a diminished sense of smell can become a picky eater. Needless to say, if you notice your older dog's food intake decreasing, schedule a visit to your veterinarian to rule out an underlying medical disorder.

Special Diets

For healthy geriatric GSPs, a high-quality ration formulated for "senior" or "older" dogs is indicated. These foods typically contain more fiber and less fat to accommodate a slowing metabolism associated with age. Increases in fiber content also serve to promote healthy bowel function in older pets. Again, stick with the same brand of food you have been feeding

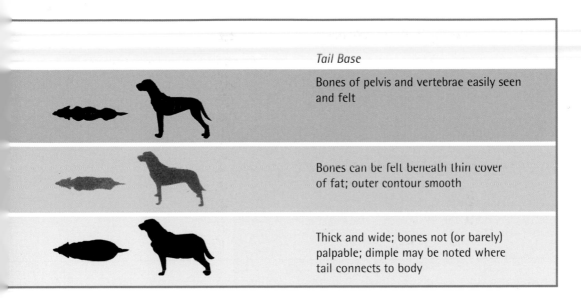

	Tail Base
	Bones of pelvis and vertebrae easily seen and felt
	Bones can be felt beneath thin cover of fat; outer contour smooth
	Thick and wide; bones not (or barely) palpable; dimple may be noted where tail connects to body

over the years to help prevent digestive upset from the transition.

✔ If your GSP is suffering from a specific illness, a special diet available from your veterinarian is needed. For example, dogs suffering from constipation, certain types of colitis, and diabetes mellitus often require fiber contents in their rations even greater than those found in standard "senior" formulas.

✔ Older dogs suffering from chronic diarrhea, excessive gas production, and/or pancreatic problems can often benefit from special diets formulated to be more easily digestible than standard maintenance rations.

✔ Recommended dietary management in dogs suffering from heart and/or kidney disease includes diets low in sodium and restricted in protein. Because prescription diets are specialized, follow your veterinarian's directions closely with regard to amounts and frequencies of feedings.

Water

Food and water bowls need to be easily accessible to older dogs, as declining vision and/or arthritic joints can make finding or reaching a bowl difficult. Keep fresh, clean water available at all times. Dogs with kidney impairment or endocrine diseases such as diabetes may drink excessive amounts of water, making refills necessary throughout the day.

Weight Control

Keeping your dog's weight under control is one of the most effective ways to add years to his life and to improve his effectiveness in the field. Obesity can be defined as an increase in body fat resulting in an increase in body weight over 10 percent the normal weight standard for the dog's breed or body type. This standard for GSPs is 55 pounds (25 kg) for smaller males; 70

pounds (32 kg) for larger ones. Female GSPs should range in weight between 45 and 60 pounds (20–27 kg), depending upon body type. Your veterinarian can help determine your dog's body type, and hence, his ideal weight.

Obesity

Obesity is undoubtedly one of the most prevalent diseases affecting dogs today. Overweight dogs are predisposed to a variety of other serious disorders such as hypertension, cardiac fatigue, pancreatitis, diabetes mellitus, and colitis. Skin disorders seem to be more prevalent in overweight dogs, as do disorders of the musculoskeletal system and nervous system, including intervertebral disc disease and osteoarthritis. Obviously, the stamina and speed of a bird dog will be adversely affected if it is carrying around excess baggage, not to mention that the chances of injury occurring in the field are greatly increased.

There is no doubt that the number one cause of obesity in dogs is dietary indiscretion; that is, feeding items other than the dog's normal food, such as table scraps. Tempted by those big, sad eyes, owners often succumb and allow these indiscretions, which only serve to pack on the pounds and create annoying beggars out of once-disciplined comrades.

If your GSP is unfashionably heavy (see Table 5), simply cutting back on the amount you feed will not provide the lasting weight loss you desire. In fact, depriving your dog of adequate amounts of food could create a state of malnutrition, leading to incessant begging and destructive behavior. The correct way to shed those extra pounds is to increase your dog's activity level and feed a ration that is specially formulated for weight loss. These diets are readily available from your veterinarian and should be fed under your clinician's direction. They generally contain a high fiber content, which allows for calorie reduction while satisfying the hunger of your pet. Feed the amount recommended on the bag that corresponds to your pet's ideal weight. If you don't know what this should be, ask your veterinarian. To keep your dog satisfied, divide the total daily ration into three or four feedings over the course of a day.

Drug: For tough cases, the drug dirlotapide (Slentrol) can be prescribed by your veterinarian to help curb your dog's appetite and limit fat absorption. This drug, when combined with a low-calorie diet, can be quite effective in helping your dog achieve his desired weight. Ask your veterinarian for details.

Performance Nutrition

GSPs that are being trained in the field or hunting require extra nutrition to counteract the additional energy expenditures needed for these activities. As a rule, working dogs will require a caloric increase of 35 to 40 percent over the amount required of the more sedentary canine; these dogs will need to extract more energy from their diet. As a result, foods fed for this purpose must be nutritionally dense and highly digestible. Foods with high energy density contain higher amounts of fat, which provides more calories per gram than do proteins or carbohydrates. Highly digestible foods refer to those rations that can be consumed in smaller amounts (compared to foods that are less digestible), while still meeting the dog's energy needs. Whenever feeding a highly dense and digestible diet, your dog should have access to plenty of water at all times. One big advantage of feeding such a diet is that your dog doesn't have to eat as much as a normal ration in order to receive adequate nutritional energy. As a result, when he begins his work, there won't be as much food in the stomach to slow him down. Dogs fed dense, highly digestible rations do not have to defecate as often, thereby avoiding another field distraction.

PREVENTIVE HEALTH CARE

A well-designed preventive health care plan can help your GSP live a long and healthy life.

A health care plan should include the following:

- Physical examinations
- Immunizations
- Intestinal parasite control
- Heartworm prevention
- Flea control
- Tick control
- Skin and coat care
- Ear care
- Dental care
- Exercise
- Elective surgeries

In addition, sound nutrition and weight control are integral parts of your dog's preventive health care program. These subjects were covered in the previous chapter.

Flea and tick control is important for your dog's health.

The Physical Examination

Although cursory physical examinations performed at home are not meant to replace routine veterinary checkups, they are quite helpful for the early detection of disease and disorders that may germinate between visits to the veterinarian. As a result, you'll want to learn how to perform one on your pet. A great time to do this exam is during your dog's regular grooming sessions. Have your veterinarian demonstrate to you how to perform a cursory physical exam on your pet at home. Table 7 provides a checklist that you can use to identify clinical signs of disease while administering the exam. If you find something abnormal, contact your veterinarian.

Immunizations

Immunizations (vaccinations) are designed to prime your GSP's immune system to protect against a variety of infectious disease agents.

Table 6: Immunization Schedule (Core Group)

Vaccine Type	Age of Initial Vaccinations	Booster Interval	Comments
Rabies	16 weeks; 1 year + 4 months	Every 1 to 3 years, depending on the state in which you live	Deadly viral disease of the central nervous system of mammals, including man; transmitted through the bite of an infected animal, also by contamination of open wounds or exposed mucous membranes; clinical signs can range from dementia and inability to swallow (foaming at the mouth) to minor behavioral changes accompanied by progressive incoordination and paralysis.
Distemper	8, 12, 16 weeks; 1 year + 4 months	Every 3 years or as recommended by your veterinarian	Widespread viral disease that affects multiple organ systems; can cause vomiting, diarrhea, pneumonia, seizures, conjunctivitis, skin disease, etc.
Parvovirus	8, 12, 16 weeks; 1 year + 4 months	Every 3 years or as recommended by your veterinarian	Highly contagious disease causing severe vomiting and bloody diarrhea; young unvaccinated puppies under 16 weeks of age most susceptible.
Adenovirus	8, 12, 16 weeks; 1 year + 4 months	Every 3 years or as recommended by your veterinarian	Viral disease of the liver and other organs transmitted between dogs through body excretions; signs include abdominal pain, jaundice, internal bleeding, and blindness ("blue eye").

Vaccinations against canine viral diseases are especially vital because, as a rule, no specific treatments exist to directly combat these agents once they gain a foothold within the dog's body.

Most puppies will receive protective antibodies from their mother's colostrum (the special "milk" secreted by the mammary glands during the first 24 hours following parturition) if the female had received immunizations prior to pregnancy. These "passive" antibodies are important because the immune system of a puppy less than six weeks of age is incapable of mounting an effective response to any disease organism. At eight weeks of age, levels of these

Table 6: Immunization Schedule (Noncore Group)

Vaccine Type	Age of Initial Vaccinations	Booster Interval	Comments
Bordetella and Parainfluenza	10 days prior to boarding, grooming, and dog shows	Intranasal vaccine every 6 months as needed	Highly contagious respiratory disease, transmitted from dog to dog by air and wind currents; classic sign is a dry, persistent cough.
Leptospirosis	As recommended by your veterinarian	As recommended by your veterinarian	Bacterial infection causing kidney and liver damage; spread through contact with water contaminated with urine from infected wildlife or livestock.
Lyme disease	As recommended by your veterinarian	As recommended by your veterinarian	Tick-borne disease affecting joints, kidneys, and other organs; humans can become infected.
Coronavirus	8 and 12 weeks or as recommended by your veterinarian	As recommended by your veterinarian	Viral disease of puppies; causes mild diarrhea, but could turn deadly in combination with parvovirus.
Porphyromonas	As recommended by your veterinarian	As recommended by your veterinarian	May help reduce the incidence of tooth and gum disease, especially in smaller breeds.
Rattlesnake Toxoid	As recommended by your veterinarian	As recommended by your veterinarian	Indicated only in high-risk hunting situations.

antibodies begin to taper off, leaving the puppy's immune system to fend for itself.

For this reason, initial vaccinations for puppies should be administered at eight weeks of age. Vaccines administered to puppies younger than eight weeks are often rendered ineffective by the passive antibodies circulating in their system and may even leave the puppies more susceptible to disease. Vaccination prior to eight weeks of age is only indicated in those instances where the mother was not current on her vaccinations prior to pregnancy, or if lack of passive antibody absorption is a possibility (for instance, if there was inadequate nursing during the first few hours of life). Unfortunately, at this age, a puppy's immune system is immature, and may not respond effectively to the immunization. As a result, extra care should

Table 7: Physical Exam Checklist
(Note: Contact your veterinarian if an abnormality is detected)

Date _____

Temperature _____ Pulse _____ Resp. _____ Weight _____

General Evaluation
- [ ] Alert
- [ ] Active
- [ ] Healthy appetite
- [ ] Playful
- [ ] Lameness
- [ ] Abnormal aggressiveness
- [ ] Disinterested
- [ ] Lethargic
- [ ] Poor appetite
- [ ] Weight loss/gain
- [ ] Abnormal posture

Skin and Hair Coat
- [ ] Appears normal
- [ ] Hair loss
- [ ] Dull; unkempt
- [ ] Scaly
- [ ] Dry
- [ ] Oily
- [ ] Itching
- [ ] Shedding
- [ ] Mats
- [ ] Tumors or warts
- [ ] Parasites
- [ ] Abnormal lumps under the skin
- [ ] Pustules

Eyes
- [ ] Appear normal
- [ ] Clear discharge
- [ ] Mucus discharge
- [ ] Redness
- [ ] Eyelid abnormalities
- [ ] Haziness/cloudiness
- [ ] Unequal pupil size
- [ ] Discoloration
- [ ] Squinting
- [ ] Protruding third eyelids

Ears
- [ ] Appear normal
- [ ] Red; swollen
- [ ] Itchy
- [ ] Creamy, yellow discharge
- [ ] Brown to black discharge
- [ ] Head shaking
- [ ] Hair loss on pinnae
- [ ] Bad odor
- [ ] Masses
- [ ] Excessive hair
- [ ] Tender
- [ ] Head tilt

Nose and Throat
- [ ] Appear normal
- [ ] Nasal discharge
- [ ] Enlarged lymph nodes (Feel on either side of the neck just under the jaw)
- [ ] Ulceration on nose
- [ ] Crusty nose

Mouth, Teeth, and Gums
- [ ] Appear normal
- [ ] Broken, discolored, or loose teeth
- [ ] Retained deciduous teeth
- [ ] Tartar accumulation
- [ ] Growths or masses
- [ ] Foul odor
- [ ] Tooth loss
- [ ] Inflamed gums
- [ ] Excess salivation
- [ ] Pale gums
- [ ] Ulcers

Miscellaneous
- [ ] Abdominal tenderness
- [ ] Coughing
- [ ] Breathing difficulties
- [ ] Abnormal stools
- [ ] Abnormal urination
- [ ] Increased water consumption
- [ ] Decreased water consumption
- [ ] Genital discharge
- [ ] Mammary lumps
- [ ] Scooting

Viral diseases are spread by close contact with infected dogs.

be taken with these puppies to prevent accidental exposure to disease agents.

Core and Noncore Vaccines

Those diseases for which your pet should be routinely vaccinated against (the "core" vaccines) include distemper, parvovirus, infectious canine hepatitis (CAV-1), and rabies. Optional (noncore) vaccines are reserved for those GSPs at a high risk of exposure due to lifestyle, geographic location, and so on. Noncore vaccines include leptospirosis, coronavirus, Bordetella,

parainfluenza, Lyme disease, and the Porphyromonas vaccine. Refer to Table 6 for recommended vaccination schedules.

Intestinal Parasite Control

To keep your GSP free of intestinal parasites such as roundworms, hookworms, and whipworms, stool checks should be performed yearly by your veterinarian. Early detection and treatment of worm infestations will help prevent malnutrition, diarrhea, and stress-related immune suppression. It will also lessen the risk of zoonotic (pet to people) transmission of these parasites, especially to children.

Heartworm Prevention

Keeping your dog on once-a-month heartworm preventive medication will also help protect against a variety of intestinal parasites, depending upon the type being given. Ask your veterinarian to recommend the best one for your individual dog.

Dirofilaria immitis, the canine heartworm, is one of the most devastating and life-threatening enemies your GSP will face during his life. Transmitted by mosquitoes, heartworms pose a risk wherever and whenever mosquitoes are found. Imagine what it would feel like to have live worms moving around within your heart and blood vessels, and you will be able to empathize with the unfortunate victims of this disease. Heartworm disease places a tremendous strain on the heart, blood vessels, lungs, liver, and kidneys, adversely affecting lifespan. Even canines kept indoors most of the time are at risk because mosquitoes can easily gain entrance into a house.

Table 8: Popular Once-a-Month Heartworm Preventive Medication

Active Ingredient	Product Name
Milbemycin	Sentinel, Interceptor
Selamectin	Revolution
Ivermectin	Heartgard, Iverhart, Triheart
Moxidectin	Advantage Multi

Fortunately, administering a special medication on a monthly basis can prevent heartworm disease. Several types and brands are available; ask your veterinarian for a recommendation (see Table 8). In warmer climates, where mosquitoes are present nearly year-round, heartworm preventive should be given year-round, whereas in those regions that experience seasonal changes and cooler temperatures, preventive medication is required during the warmer "mosquito" months. Consult your veterinarian as to the proper preventive medication schedule to follow in your particular area.

If your dog is not currently on a heartworm prevention program, call right now and schedule an appointment with your veterinarian to start him on one. A blood test will be required prior to starting your dog on a preventive medication to be sure that he has not already been exposed to this parasite.

Flea Control

By far the most common external parasite that your GSP will encounter is the flea. This parasite, whose bite can cause either localized irritation or a more generalized allergic reaction, is also the carrier of the common dog tapeworm, *Dipylidium caninum*. As a result, diligent flea control should be given top priority. This includes treating not only your dog, but also your house and yard as well.

Flea Control Products

When treating your dog, keep in mind that dips and shampoos have little residual effect and are not especially useful for long-term flea control. Instead, plan on using one of the several new flea control products that have reached the market in recent years (see Table 9).

✔ Fipronil (Frontline) kills adult fleas on dogs and helps to break the flea lifecycle by killing immature fleas before they can lay eggs. This product is also effective against ticks. Applied as a spray or topical solution, fipronil collects within the hair follicles and sebaceous glands of the skin, providing good residual action after initial application.

✔ Imidacloprid (Advantage, Advantix) and selamectin (Revolution) are two more weapons in the flea control arsenal. Both are designed to be applied monthly to the dog's back as topical drops and both work by killing adult fleas on contact. It should be noted that imidacloprid may be rendered ineffective by frequent bathing.

✔ Lufenuron (Program, Sentinel) is a product designed to be taken internally by your GSP. Available in tablet form, lufenuron exerts its flea control action by sterilizing the fleas that

bite the dog, thereby rendering those fleas sterile. Because they cannot reproduce, fleas are eventually eliminated (in a contained environment) via attrition. Lufenuron does not actually kill adult fleas. As a result, products that kill adult fleas should be used in conjunction with this treatment in order to achieve effective flea

Table 9: Popular Flea Products

Generic Name	Trade Name Products	Advantages	Disadvantages
Fipronil	Frontline	Does not wash off with bathing (unless bathed within 48 hrs of application); kills ticks.	Occasional skin irritation at application site; do not use on pets under 10 weeks or pregnant dogs.
Imidacloprid	Advantage, Advantix	Kills flea larvae as well as adults.	Washes off with bathing.
Selamectin	Revolution	Also prevents heartworms; kills mange mites and certain ticks; safe for pregnant dogs.	Occasional skin irritation at application site.
Lufenuron	Program, Sentinel	Oral tablet; easy to administer.	Sterilizes, but doesn't kill adult fleas.

CHECKLIST

Removing Ticks

1. Never attempt to remove ticks from your dog by applying manual pressure alone, or by applying a hot match or needle to the tick's body.
2. Most ticks first killed by the application of a pyrethrin spray will fall off with time once they die. In some cases, you may need to manually remove the dead tick after spraying.
3. When picking one off your dog, never use your bare hands in order to prevent accidental exposure to disease.
4. Use gloves and tweezers to grasp the dead tick as close to its attachment site as possible, then pull straight up using constant tension until the tick is freed.
5. Wash the bite wound with soap and water and apply a first aid cream or ointment to prevent infection.

control. As one might expect, many veterinarians recommend this product for those dogs kept in an indoor (contained) environment and who do not suffer from allergies to fleas.

Home Premises Treatment

Home premises treatment is best accomplished by sprinkling orthoboric acid powder on the carpets and near the baseboards of your home. Noticeable results are usually obtained within a week after application. Odorless, easy to use, and safe for pets and children, orthoboric acid is available under various brand names from your local pet supply store. Under normal conditions, application of this product must be performed every six to twelve months. Carpets must remain dry for continued efficacy; if the carpet becomes damp or is shampooed, reapplication will be necessary.

Finally, your yard should be treated with insecticide granules every six to eight weeks during the warm months of the year. Fleas will proliferate in warm, dark, moist environments, so treat around hedges, under decks, and in some cases, under the house itself.

Tick Control

Measures used to control ticks on your dog are similar to those used to control fleas. Fipronil (Frontline) is an excellent product that can be used to control both fleas and ticks. If your pet frequents environments heavily infested with ticks, a flea and tick collar can help keep these parasites away from the face and ears. In addition, a pyrethrin spray can be applied to your dog's haircoat prior to a trip to the field to discourage ticks from attaching. If a few happen to slip by, use the same pyrethrin spray to kill those that have attached to the skin.

Seed Ticks

Female ticks will lay their eggs in and under sheltered areas in your yard, such as wood stumps, rocks, and wall crevices. Once hatched, the larvae, called "seed ticks," will crawl up onto grass stems or bushes and attach themselves to your dog if he happens to pass by. As a result, thorough and consistent treatment of the yard with an approved acaricide is needed to adequately control tick populations. Because ticks can live for months in their surrounding

habitat without a blood meal, yard treatment should be performed every four weeks during the peak tick season in your area.

Skin and Coat Care

Grooming is an important part of any preventive health care program. Not only will it help keep your dog in top shape physically, but the time spent with your GSP will provide much psychological comfort. As an added benefit, routine grooming and hands-on attention will assist in the early detection of external parasites, tumors, infections, or any other changes or abnormalities that may result from internal disease.

Brushing and Bathing

As a rule, if you brush your GSP on a daily basis, the need for bathing is minimal. Routine bathing should be performed only on those dogs that are continually being exposed to excessive dirt, grease, or other noxious substances in their environment, and for those canines suffering from external parasites or medical conditions such as infections and/or seborrhea of the skin.

If a general cleaning is desired for an otherwise healthy dog, then the best recommendation is to purchase and use a mild hypoallergenic shampoo for this purpose. These shampoos are readily available from your veterinarian or favorite pet supply store. If your dog is afflicted with any type of medical condition, then the type of shampoo used should be limited to that recommended or prescribed by your veterinarian.

Prior to giving your dog a bath, apply some type of protection to both eyes to prevent corneal burns if shampoo accidentally gets into the eyes. Mineral oil can be used for this purpose;

however, a sterile ophthalmic ointment is preferred. Such an ointment can be purchased from your veterinarian or pet store.

Nail Care

Your pointer's nails should be examined every three to four weeks and trimmed at that time, if necessary. Overgrown, neglected nails will snag and tear easily, causing pain and discomfort. Additionally, nail overgrowth can lead to gait instability and joint stress, two complications that your dog does not need.

To determine whether or not your pointer's nails are too long, observe the paws as they rest flat on the floor with your dog standing. If any nail touches the floor surface, it is a candidate for trimming.

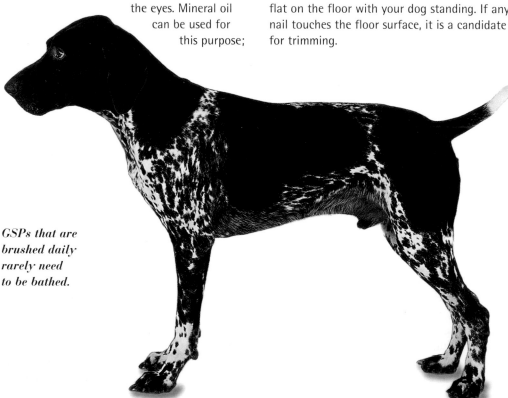

GSPs that are brushed daily rarely need to be bathed.

Trimming

✔ When trimming nails, use only a brand of nail clipper that is designed for dogs. If your dog's nails are clear, you should be able to note the line of demarcation between the pink quick (the portion of the nail that contains the blood supply) and the remaining portions of the nails.

✔ Snip off the latter portion just in front of the quick. For those GSPs with darker nails, use a flashlight or penlight beam to illuminate the quick portion prior to trimming.

✔ If this still doesn't enable you to visualize the quick, trim off only small portions at a time until the nail is no longer bearing weight.

✔ Although ideally you want to avoid drawing blood when you are trimming your dog's nails, don't fret if you do so. Using a clean cloth or towel, simply apply direct pressure to the end of the bleeding nail for three to five minutes. In most cases, this is all that is needed to stop the bleeding.

✔ For stubborn cases, commercially available clotting powder can be applied to the end of the nail to help stop the hemorrhage.

Ear Care

Because the canine external ear canal is long, and because the earflaps of GSPs are pendulous, routine care for the ears is needed to prevent moisture, wax, and debris from accumulating. This involves cleaning and drying the ears on a bimonthly basis.

Many different types of ear cleansers and drying agents are readily available from pet stores, pet supply houses, and veterinary offices. Liquid ear cleansers are preferred over powders because the latter tend to saturate with moisture and trap it within the ear canal. Most liq-

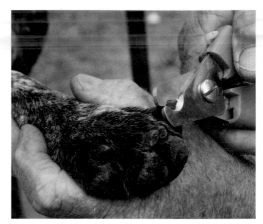

Nail trims are an integral part of any grooming program.

uid ear cleansers contain both a wax solvent and drying agent (astringent) that clean the ear and dry it at the same time.

Prior to cleaning your dog's ears, take note of any signs of irritation, discharges, or foul odors. If one or all are noted, your pet's ears should be examined by your veterinarian in lieu of cleaning. This is recommended as well for dogs that appear to be constantly shaking or tilting their heads. The reason for this is that unhealthy ears may have torn or diseased eardrums, and introducing a cleansing solution into such an ear can spread infection to the deeper portions of the ear.

Cleaning the Ears

Assuming your dog's ears are healthy, begin cleaning by gently pulling the earflap out and away from the head, exposing and straightening the ear canal. Carefully squeeze a liberal amount of ear-cleaning solution into the ear and massage the ear canal for 20 seconds. Next, allow your dog to shake his head, then proceed

Good dental health can add years to your dog's life.

to the opposite ear and follow the same procedure. Once both ears have been treated, use cotton balls or swabs to remove any wax or debris found on the inside folds of the earflap and the outer portions of the ear canal. To avoid serious injury to your dog's ear, never enter into the actual ear canal when swabbing.

Dental Care

Keeping your GSP's teeth free of tartar and plaque buildup is a preventive health care procedure that will in itself add years to the life of your GSP. It is estimated that tooth and gum disease (periodontal disease) strikes over 85 percent of all dogs by three years of age. Not only do plaque-laden teeth and inflamed gums lead to halitosis (foul breath) and eventual tooth loss, but bacteria from these sources can enter the bloodstream and travel to the heart and kidneys, where they can set up an infec-

tion. Infection of the heart valves and subsequent heart failure can all too often be traced back to periodontal disease. As a result, regular visits to your veterinarian for professional cleaning and polishing, supplemented by an at-home dental care program, are a must to keep your dog's teeth, and heart, healthy.

Professional Cleaning

Because a short-acting sedative/ anesthetic will be required for professional cleaning, blood tests should be performed on your dog prior to anesthesia to make certain that there are no underlying conditions that may complicate recovery. Once anesthetized, an ultrasonic scaler is used to shatter and break up the plaque that has accumulated on your dog's teeth above and below the gum line. After this has been completed, the mouth is rinsed and a polisher is used on the teeth to restore their smooth, shiny surfaces. The entire procedure should take no more than 30 to 40 minutes, after which time your pet will be recovered from the anesthesia.

Toothpastes and Cleaning Solutions

Professional teeth cleaning such as that described above may be required every other year; however, with diligent dental care provided by you at home on a daily basis, this interval can be extended. Toothpastes and cleansing solutions designed for dogs are available from your veterinarian or local pet stores. For best results, use preparations that contain chlorhexidine, an antimicrobial agent that can provide hours of residual protection against bacteria that may attempt to colonize the tooth and gum surfaces.

Note: Do not use toothpastes designed for use in humans on your dog; these can

Brush daily if possible.

cause severe stomach upset in your GSP if swallowed.

A soft-bristled toothbrush or cloth should be used to gently massage the paste or solution onto the outer surfaces of the teeth and gums. If in doubt, ask your veterinarian to demonstrate the safe and correct procedure for brushing your dog's teeth.

Devices

Special devices designed to help keep your dog's teeth free of tartar can also be used to supplement your efforts at home. Certain rawhide, nylon, and urethane chew bones are specially designed to massage and clean a dog's teeth while he is chewing on the device. In addition, flossing devices are commercially available that can help reduce tartar buildup more than brushing alone.

Vaccine

A vaccine is now available to help in the fight against periodontal disease. The Porphyromonas vaccine may help build immunity against the most common organisms that cause decay and bone loss within the oral cavity. Ask your pet health professional for details on these and other methods for keeping your pointer's teeth and gums disease-free.

Exercising Your German Shorthaired Pointer

A moderate exercise program included in your GSP's daily routine will reap multiple health benefits for him. It will improve his cardiovascular endurance and function, allowing him to go long distances for long periods of time, which can be of great benefit on a busy all-day hunt. Physical exercise helps tone and tighten the muscles and improve recovery times, allowing your dog to go longer and harder during the hunt. For GSPs not used for hunting, it will help maintain muscle tone and strength in otherwise sedentary dogs. Exercise will also improve your dog's agility and flexibility, and help loosen up any stiff joints. Regular exercise will also promote and improve gastrointestinal motility, stimulating nutrient absorption and ensuring maximum utilization. Finally, keeping your dog physically fit will help keep his weight in check, preventing obesity and all of the health ramifications that come with it (see Obesity page 34).

Exercise Tips

Before implementing any exercise program for your GSP, a complete physical exam should be performed by your veterinarian to identify any underlying health conditions that may limit the type and amount of exercise performed. Follow your veterinarian's advice closely in designing a fitness program around the special needs of your individual pet.

There are several avenues to take in order to heighten and strengthen your GSP's cardiovascular endurance and muscle fitness.

✔ Swimming is great exercise and can often be combined with retrieval training. It is especially useful for increasing cardiovascular endurance and toning certain muscle groups.

✔ Owing to the size of GSPs, they also make great walking or jogging partners; however, check with your doctor before you undertake such a program yourself.

✔ Allow a 10-minute cool-down following any strenuous activity.

✔ Provide your GSP access to plenty of fresh water to allow for replacement of fluids lost due to physical exertion.

✔ Isotonic sport drinks or electrolyte formulas available from your local food store are also effective means of replenishing lost fluids and electrolytes.

Physical Conditioning for Hunting Season

About 60 days prior to the beginning of hunting season you should plan on implementing a conditioning program for both you and your dog in order to prepare physically for the big days that lie ahead. As far as your dog's conditioning program is concerned, plan on gradually increasing the number of trips into the field as time permits. Ideally, if you can get your dog into the field three to five times weekly for 45 to 90 minutes at a time, he will undoubtedly be in top condition when hunting season arrives. Beginning a conditioning program early will also allow time for your dog's foot pads to toughen and to prepare for the rough fields and woods he is likely to encounter in the days to come.

Elective Surgeries

An elective surgery is a surgical procedure designed to improve the health and/or function of the individual in question. There are three elective surgeries often performed on GSPs. These include neutering, tail docking, and removal of the dewclaws.

Neutering Your Pet

The term "neutering" refers to the removal of the ovaries and uterus (ovariohysterectomy) in the female dog or the testicles (castration) in the male. Because of the high incidence of reproductive disorders in older dogs, including uterine infections and prostate disorders, it is recommended that neutering be performed at a young age before these problems arise. In females, neutering prior to the second heat cycle can dramatically reduce the risk of mammary cancer at a later age.

Contrary to popular belief, neutering your dog won't lead to laziness and obesity; there are many examples of slim and trim neutered dogs that debunk this myth. Improper feeding practices, lack of exercise, and, in some instances, metabolic disorders cause obesity in dogs, not reproductive status. Furthermore, although it is true that neutering can have a calming effect on nervous or restless GSPs, activity levels in emotionally stable dogs are rarely affected.

Tail Docking and Dewclaw Removal

Established conformational standards dictate that select breeds of dogs, including GSPs, have artificially shortened tails and be free of dewclaws. Tail docking originated in centuries past as a way to prevent hunting and sporting dogs from traumatizing their tails while working in thick woods or underbrush.

Dewclaws are actually functionless remnants of the first digit on each paw. Many puppies are born without any dewclaws at all; others may be born with them on the front paws, but not the back, or vice versa. Dewclaws have a nasty habit of getting snagged and torn on carpet, furniture, and in sporting dogs such as GSPs, underbrush. Secondary infections can develop if this trauma is repeated. For this reason, removal of dewclaws is indicated.

Tail docking and dewclaw removal are best performed within the first week of life, and simply involve snipping off the dewclaws and the desired length of tail (per breed standards) with scissors. One to two sutures are usually placed in the tail; the site of the dewclaw removal is often cauterized and left open to heal. If tail docking and dewclaw removal are not performed within seven days after birth, anesthesia will be required for the surgery. As a result, the procedures will have to be postponed until the dog is five to six months of age and can tolerate anesthesia.

If you encounter a sudden injury or illness affecting your GSP either at home or in the field, don't panic—this will only hinder your first aid efforts. The ultimate goal of any first aid is simple: to stabilize your dog's condition until professional medical care can be obtained.

Bleeding

To control bleeding, you should immediately apply direct pressure to the source of the hemorrhage. Any readily available absorbable material or object can be used as a compress, including gauze, towels, or shirts. For your own safety, muzzle your dog prior to doing so.

Pressure should be applied for no less than five minutes. If bleeding still persists after this time, secure the compress using gauze, a belt, pantyhose, or a necktie, and seek veterinary help immediately. If an extremity is involved, pressure applied to the inside, upper portion of the affected leg will also reduce blood flow to the limb. If needed, a tourniquet may be applied just *above* the wound, using a belt, necktie, or pantyhose. A pencil, ruler, or wooden spoon can be used to twist and tighten the tourniquet until bleeding has been minimized. To prevent permanent damage to the limb, you should be able to pass one finger between the

tourniquet and the skin without too much effort. In addition, release tourniquet pressure for 30 seconds every 10 to 15 minutes until veterinary care is obtained.

Poisonings

General symptoms associated with a poisoning include vomiting, diarrhea, unconsciousness, seizures, abdominal pain, excessive salivation, panting, and/or shock. Common sources of poisoning in dogs include house plants, rodent poisons, insecticides, chocolate, ethylene glycol (anti-freeze), drug overdose, and ingestion of spoiled or denatured food.

Goals of first aid treatment for poisoning should be geared toward diluting or neutralizing the poison as much as possible prior to veterinary intervention. If the poison originated from a container, always read and follow the label directions concerning accidental poisoning. In addition, take the label and container with you to your veterinarian.

If your dog has ingested a caustic or petroleum-based substance, or is severely depressed, seizing, or unconscious, waste no time in seek-

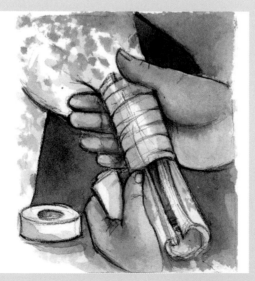

Applying a temporary splint using a rolled-up magazine and gauze.

ing veterinary help. Treatment in these instances should be administered only under a veterinarian's guidance.

For other ingested poisons, induce vomiting using a teaspoon per 10 pounds (4.5 kg) of body weight of hydrogen peroxide. Repeat in five minutes if needed.

Following evacuation of the stomach, administer two cups of water orally to help dilute any remaining poison. If available, administer activated charcoal (mix 25 grams of powder in water to form a slurry, then administer one ml per pound of body weight) or whole milk (one cup) to help deactivate any residual poison.

If the poison was applied to the skin, flush the affected areas with copious amounts of water. If the offending substance is oil-based, a bath using water plus a mechanic's hand cleaner or dishwashing liquid should be given to remove any remaining residue.

Note: In all instances of poisoning, specific antidotes may be available at your veterinarian's office. As a result, always seek out professional care following initial first aid efforts.

Bone Fractures

Signs of a fractured bone will include abnormal limb position or mobility, localized pain, bruising, and/or crepitation (the crackling feel made when two ends of bone rub together). If the fracture is open; that is, the ends of the bone are protruding through the skin, do not attempt to replace the exposed ends of bone or clean the wound.

Start by putting a muzzle on your dog. Control any bleeding that may be present and apply a clean or sterile bandage to the site prior to transporting your dog to your veterinarian. If the fracture is closed and is suspected

Table 10: Items to Include in a First Aid Kit

- Antibiotic cream or ointment
- Bandage scissors
- Betadine solution
- Cotton balls
- Digital thermometer
- Elastic bandages
- Hydrogen peroxide 3% solution
- Saline solution
- Snake bite kit
- Sterile nonstick dressings
- Sterile ophthalmic ointment
- Tongue depressors
- Tourniquet
- Tweezers
- Two-inch adhesive tape
- Two-inch gauze roll

below the dog's elbow or knee, immobilize it by applying a splint to the affected region. A rolled-up magazine affixed to the limb with adhesive tape or cloth makes an excellent splint. Other materials that can be used as splints include sticks, rulers, and small boards. Be careful not to apply any tape directly over the fracture site. Once the fracture is splinted, carefully transport your GSP to your veterinarian at once for further stabilization.

Table 11: Normal Physiologic Values for the Shorthair

Temperature	Pulse (beats per minute)	Respirations (per minute)
99.5–102.2°F (37.5–39°C)	60–120	14–22

UNDERSTANDING YOUR GERMAN SHORTHAIRED POINTER

GSPs possess an intelligence that makes them sometimes act almost human. They can also exhibit a tremendous amount of free will and stubbornness if they so choose.

Knowing how to apply a little "dog" psychology to our GSPs will help enhance the relationship we have with them and help us deal with behavioral problems that may sometimes arise. Before we can utilize such remedies, however, we must first have a basic understanding of the canine learning process that makes them act the way they do.

Apart from inherent instinctive reactions, canine behavior is influenced by two dominant factors: sensory perception and learning intelligence.

Sensory Perception

As you can guess, dogs perceive their world differently than we do. This is vital to remember, especially when training them because, in

GSPs are highly intelligent dogs.

our own perception, we may not completely understand certain responses and behaviors that we see in them. However, by learning how GSPs perceive their world with their senses, the reasons become clearer.

Sight

The visual acuity of the dog is about the same as that of a human around dusk or nightfall; in other words, images seen are more general than specific. If you've ever worn a new hat or sunglasses around your GSP, only to have it back away from you or bark in apprehension, he did so because he didn't recognize the specifics of your "new look."

Smell

By far the most important sense for a dog is the sense of smell. The canine brain has almost ten times more area devoted to this sense than does the human brain. As a result, canine noses are so acute that it's impossible to artificially mask a scent from them. Such a keen sense of smell will obviously have a definite bearing on behavior in certain instances.

Hearing

The sense of hearing in the average dog is much more fine-tuned than that of a human, allowing him to detect much higher sound pitches at a wider range of frequencies. The upper range of canine hearing is thought to be around 47,000 cycles per second, almost 30,000 cycles per second higher than that of humans. This means that even with its long, pendulous

earflaps, the GSP has no problem detecting and reacting to a plethora of sounds that we can't even begin to hear.

Taste

Ever wondered why some dogs, when fed table scraps, become incessant beggars? The answer lies in their tongues, which contain a high proportion of taste buds that respond to sugars and certain "sweet" amino acids. In essence, your GSP can quickly develop a "sweet tooth" if fed improperly. Some dogs will even go so far as to refuse well-balanced rations for the sweeter "junk" food. The ramifications of this with regard to the health and performance of your dog are obvious. As a result, to prevent bad habits from forming, avoid the temptation to consistently sneak your pal snacks between meals.

Learning Intelligence

Habituation

In addition to actions prompted by instinct and by sensory input, dog behavior is governed heavily by learning intelligence. The most basic type of learning exhibited by dogs is habituation, characterized by a diminishing response to a stimulus that is repeated over and over. This type of learning comes in quite handy when trying to manage separation anxiety in a pet (see Solving Behavioral Challenges, page 69).

Associative Learning

Another type of learning in dogs is called associative learning, where the dog created mental links between two or more different types of actions, results, and/or stimuli. For instance, rewarding your dog for a job well done during a training session will create a mental link in his brain, where he associates the action with pleasure. The more times the specific action/reward cycle is repeated, the stronger the link becomes.

Associative learning, as well as other more complex learning patterns, also influences socialization.

Socialization

By far the most important time in the life of your GSP puppy is between the ages of three and twelve weeks. During this "socialization period," young GSPs link social acceptance or hostility to members of their own species, as well as to other species. For example, if for some reason a puppy fails to be properly introduced to other dogs, cats, or humans

during this time, there is a good chance that he will not get along with them as an adult. The same holds true for those young puppies that experience some traumatic, negative event involving another animal or human. For example, if a male owner abuses a puppy during the socialization period, he may grow up to have an intense aversion to all men. Also, if a puppy does not have contact with children during peak socialization, he may not recognize them as "human" and fail to treat them with the same respect and friendliness as he does adults.

This socialization is so important that whenever you are purchasing a GSP older than 12 weeks of age, always question the seller about the puppy's socialization experiences and about the specific steps that the seller took to ensure that proper socialization indeed took place. If proper socialization

did not take place, you may be faced with unexpected behavioral challenges in the future.

Important Training Principles

✔ To achieve fast and lasting results from your training efforts, you will need to use plenty of patience, consistency, and repetition. Young puppies, and even many adult GSPs, have very short attention spans. As a result, expect training progress to be made incrementally over multiple, brief training sessions. For instance, four 15-minute sessions per day will yield more fruitful results than will two 30-minute training sessions. This will no doubt require plenty of patience and dedication on your part.

✔ For best results, schedule training sessions immediately upon arriving home from work and prior to leaving for work. Your pet will be excited to have you home from work and will link the training experience to his pleasure at being reunited with you.

✔ In addition, dogs are very receptive to learning after waking from a deep sleep. A good training session prior to leaving for work will also give your dog a good dose of activity that may serve to reduce his anxiety upon your departure.

✔ To bring consistency to your efforts, hold your training sessions at the same time each day, and plan on administering your commands each time using the same voice tone, voice inflection pattern, and body language. Your dog will hear your words as sounds without verbal understanding, but he will soon learn to recognize those sounds, based upon the above criteria, and mentally link them to the corresponding action that resulted in a reward.

Double Standards

Avoid double standards in your approach to training your dog, as these cause confusion. For example, if you are going to allow your dog to sleep with you on your bed, don't get upset when you find hair all over your other furniture. Along the same lines, if you allow your GSP to jump on you when you are wearing old jeans and a T-shirt, how can you reprimand him for jumping on you when you are wearing a business suit? In other words, set the standards of behavior for your dog and stick to them.

Repetition

Finally, along with patience and consistency, repetition will help to ensure positive training outcomes. Repeating a command and subsequent action over and over will quickly create reinforcement in your dog's mind. In addition, for those GSPs that have mastered their basic training, offer brief refresher courses at least once a week for the remainder of their lives. In dogs, as in people, repetition is indeed the "mother of skill."

Praise and Reward

For quickest results when training, use praise and reward for a job well done instead of punishment for a job done poorly. Punishment serves only to create anxiety and neurosis. After all, a dog's instinctive desire is to please, not to anger its pack leader. Make it easy for your dog to "win" so you can be sure there will be plenty of praise and reward doled out during the training session.

Bear in mind that many mistakes are made out of confusion, misunderstanding, or lack of ability rather than out of disobedience. Your

companion wants to please you; he just may not know how to do it right now. It's your job to show him how. Once you do, you'll soon have your dog consistently performing up to your expectations.

Establishing Dominance

It is important to establish your dominance in your relationship with your dog right from the start. There are four ways to do it while you are training, keeping in mind that the younger the dog is, the more likely it is that he will submit to your authority.

1. Maintaining control of your dog's head and neck region using a collar (or head halter) and lead is the first way to assert your dominance. A dog is naturally protective of its neck region because this is the first place an opponent will target during a fight. By gaining control of this region with the collar and leash, your dog will have no choice but to submit to your higher authority.

2. A second way to establish your dominance is to apply downward pressure along your dog's back. In the wild, dogs assert their dominance over one another by mounting each other's back region. By simply petting your dog along his neck and back regions, you are in essence asserting your dominance, just as his wild peers do. Plus, your GSP will like the attention.

3. A third method for asserting dominance is to establish direct eye contact with your dog whenever signaling or giving a command. This is a game of "the first one to look away loses," so be sure that you never lose.

4. Finally, by staying calm and relaxed during your training sessions, your dog will sense that you are in control. Dogs can readily sense nervousness and stress in their handlers and yours won't hesitate to take advantage of the situation if he thinks he can. Unfortunately, if he succeeds, reestablishing your rightful rank may be difficult. As a result, always carry with you an air of confidence and control whenever you are around your dog.

YOUR DOG'S BASIC TRAINING

Your GSP's basic training consists of three types: house-training, desensitization training, and obedience training. For more information on house-training, see HOW-TO: House-train Your Puppy, page 26.

All three types of basic training can be started as early as eight weeks of age. Keep in mind that anything that your dog learns, good or bad, between the ages of eight and sixteen weeks (coined the "period of stable learning") will become firmly entrenched in his mind for the remainder of his life.

Desensitization Training

Desensitization training is often overlooked by a new dog owner, yet it can be one of the most valuable tools for preventing behavioral problems as a dog matures. There are three categories of desensitization training:

1. Contact desensitization
2. Separation desensitization
3. Noise desensitization.

Proper obedience training can curb many behavioral problems.

The first two categories should be addressed starting at eight weeks of age and the third at sixteen weeks.

Contact

Contact desensitization training will condition your GSP to allow his feet, ears, and mouth region to be handled. This is vitally important for your pet's preventive health care program, as such permission afforded to you will allow you to trim nails, clean ears, and brush your pet's teeth without a fight. When interacting with your puppy, make a special effort to gently touch and handle these regions with your fingers several times a day. Don't attempt to actually trim nails, brush teeth, or clean ears; instead, simply go through the motions. Soon, your puppy won't think twice when you reach out and grasp a paw or an earflap. Just remember to temporarily discontinue your efforts if a struggle ensues. Any

Separation

The goal of separation desensitization training is to desensitize your puppy to being left alone by himself. This important exercise will help prevent a common behavioral disorder seen in GSPs—separation anxiety (see page 69). This type of desensitization can be achieved by putting your puppy in his travel kennel and leaving the house for a predetermined period of time (a few minutes at a time for the first day, then gradually working up over several weeks to 20 or 30 minutes each day), being careful not to make a fuss over your puppy or respond to his protests prior to your leaving. In addition, when you reenter the house, wait several minutes before you let your puppy out of his kennel, doing your best to ignore his pleas. When you do finally let him out, take him immediately outside to use the bathroom area. Act as though your arrivals and departures are "nothing special" and your puppy will soon acquiesce to being left alone.

Strange or Loud Noises

The third type of desensitization training to start at an early age is the desensitization to strange or loud noises. The easiest method for accomplishing this training is to regularly expose your puppy to recordings of various sounds, such as the sound of thunderstorms, fireworks, or in the case of hunting dogs, gunfire. Compact discs containing these sounds are available at most book and record stores, or can be tracked down over the Internet. Playing these recordings in the presence of your puppy for 15 minutes daily (start at a very low volume and steadily increase it over a period of three to six weeks) can help achieve the desired desensitization.

negative or painful experience involving these regions during your initial training efforts can produce the exact opposite effect and create an individual that will struggle vehemently when attempts are made to perform these simple procedures.

Obedience Training

In addition to desensitization training and house-training, obedience training should also be initiated around eight weeks of age. Obedience training involves the teaching of basic verbal commands that will allow you to control your GSP in any given setting.

Equipment

Equipment you will need for obedience training your GSP includes a clicker, reward treats, head halter, retractable leash, and a travel kennel.

The clicker: The clicker is an inexpensive handheld device that generates a distinct and unique "click" sound when pressed between the thumb and finger. This auditory signal is used to capture the attention of a canine student the instant he performs a desired action. The click is always followed by a "secondary" reward, such as a food treat. Pick up some tasty reward treats at the same time you purchase your clicker.

Training with a clicker: Training with a clicker relies on associative learning to achieve results. Dogs associate the click sound with the food treat and thereby perform primarily for the signal, not the treat. Because the signal is linked instantaneously with the desired behavior, there is never any confusion in your dog's mind as to which behavior led to the "click," and thereby the treat.

Head halter: A head halter is invaluable for teaching your dog to heel and walk on a leash, allowing you full control of the head. If your dog attempts to pull away from you, the halter will pull the head down and prevent your dog from continuing on.

Retractable leash: The retractable leash will come in handy for teaching your dog to *heel*

CHECKLIST

Training Principles

✔ Keep initial training sessions short, frequent, and to the point to hold the attention of your student.

✔ The instant your dog performs the desired behavior, cue (if applicable, with a verbal command), signal (with clicker or whistle), and treat.

✔ Always end your training session with a positive result.

✔ If a particular training session isn't going well, go back to a command your dog has previously learned and end the session on a positive note.

✔ Plan on reinforcing your dog's basic training at least one day per week for the remainder of his life. In most instances, you'll be able to eventually wean your dog off the clicker in lieu of the verbal cue.

(see page 65) and for controlling range during field training. These leashes can be purchased in variable sizes and lengths at pet stores, discount stores, Internet retailers, and through mail order catalogs.

Travel kennel: The travel kennel you choose should be large enough for your dog to turn around in, yet small enough to prevent unnecessary movement during transport. You may end up having to purchase an additional kennel as your dog matures, as he may soon outgrow the original carrier you purchased for him when he was a puppy.

Getting Started

Seven essential obedience commands your dog needs to learn include *sit*, *stay*, *down*, *come*, *stop*, *heel*, and *kennel*. GSPs are quite intelligent and most puppies will pick up these commands quite easily.

Remember these important training principles when teaching obedience commands:

To begin, prime your dog to the clicker. To do this:

• Position yourself in front of your dog and make eye contact. The instant this eye contact is made, signal (click), and treat.
• Look away and wait 10 seconds, then reestablish eye contact.
• Signal and treat.
• Repeat this process over a three- to five-minute period. You'll soon find that your dog will actively seek out eye contact with you.
• Now reinforce your pet's name by making eye contact, then saying your dog's name. Signal and treat right away.
• Practice this exercise several times a day until the desired response is firmly ingrained in your dog's psyche. Your dog should now make eye contact with you whenever his name is called and/or when the signal is given.

Once you feel confident that your dog is primed to your auditory signal, proceed with the following obedience commands:

Sit

✔ Position your dog in front of you, facing you, and make eye contact. Signal and treat.
✔ With a treat in hand, hold it over the back of your dog's head and slowly lower it. Your dog should instinctively assume the sitting position. If your dog insists on backing up instead of sitting, you may have to position him

Table 12: Training Equipment

• Collar
• Head halter
• Retractable leash
• Clicker
• Food treats/rewards
• Travel kennel

in front of a door or a wall to prevent him from backing up.
✔ The instant your dog sits, say "*Sit*," then signal and treat. Keep your hand low to his head so he will remain in the sitting position.
✔ Repeat until your dog remains seated for at least 10 seconds at a time.

Stay

✔ Instruct your dog to *sit*, then, without moving, pause for several seconds before you signal and treat. Repeat this exercise multiple times, working up to a 10-second pause before you signal and treat.
✔ Next, have your dog sit and pause again for 10 seconds. Then hold up your hand and say "*Stay*," then signal and treat.
✔ Practice at random pause intervals until your dog performs correctly at least eight consecutive times, then practice moving backward and from side to side, then returning to your original position. Whenever your dog maintains his sitting posture for at least 10 seconds, signal and treat.

Down

✔ Position your dog in front of you, facing you, and make eye contact. Signal and treat.
✔ With a treat in hand, lower it slowly to the ground just in front of your pet's muzzle. Your

dog should instinctively lie down in order to get the treat. When he does, say *"Down,"* followed by a signal and treat.

✔ Repeat the exercise until your dog remains in the *down* position for at least 10 seconds.

Come

✔ Position your dog facing you and make eye contact. Signal and treat.

✔ With an additional treat in hand, have him *stay*, signal and treat, then repeat the command and move backward a short distance.

✔ Drop the treat on the ground in front of you to lure your dog toward you. When he moves, say *"Come,"* then signal and treat. Be sure your dog is able to find the treat to complete the reward.

✔ Repeat the exercise at varying distances.

Stop

✔ Take your dog for a walk with the retractable lead attached to his head halter.

✔ As he begins to distance himself from you on the lead, give a verbal *"Stop"* and tug gently on the head halter. If he stops, immediately signal and treat.

✔ Repeat the exercise as often as needed. When you feel your GSP has mastered the command, try it without the lead (always within the confines of a restricted area, such as a fenced yard).

Heel

✔ With head halter and retractable lead in place, position yourself on your GSP's left side facing forward, with his shoulders even with your knee.

✔ Give a quick forward tug on the lead, say *"Heel,"* and start forward, with your left foot leading. The instant your dog moves, signal and treat.

✔ Gradually increase the distances you walk with your dog before stopping. Signal and treat for desired behavior.

✔ Once your dog has become comfortable walking in straight lines by your side, take it through some turns to both the right and the left. During the turns, your dog's shoulder should remain aligned with your knee. Signal and treat when earned.

Kennel

✔ Position your dog in front of his travel carrier and have him *sit*. Signal and treat.

✔ Open the door to the carrier and toss a treat inside. When your dog moves and enters the carrier to get it, say *"Kennel,"* followed by a signal and another treat. Repeat several times. If needed, don't hesitate to gently "guide" your dog into the carrier with your hands.

✔ Next, position your dog several feet away from its travel carrier (door open) and have him *stay*. Signal and treat.

✔ Hold up the treat so that your dog can see it, then toss it into the carrier. When your dog enters the kennel to get it, say *"Kennel,"* followed by a signal and another treat.

✔ Repeat until your dog enters the carrier without hesitation.

SOLVING BEHAVIORAL CHALLENGES

Nothing can do more to dampen the bond you share with your dog than behavioral challenges. The bad news is that addressing behavioral problems takes time and effort on your part. The good news is that most can be brought under control through the use of special techniques and/or therapy. By allowing your veterinarian to play an active role in the treatment process, you will increase the chances of success a hundredfold.

Separation Anxiety

Have you ever left the house, sometimes for only a few minutes, and your "best friend" proceeds to chew up the furniture, bark or howl, and/or eliminate in the house? If your dog behaves this way when you leave your home, he is probably suffering from the behavioral problem known as "separation anxiety." Before a problem like separation anxiety can be successfully treated, it is helpful to know what causes it.

Dogs are considered "pack animals"; that is, they prefer to run in groups rather than indi-

Separation anxiety is a frustrating behavioral disorder.

vidually. Being his owner, a dog will consider you part of his "pack" and will constantly want to associate with you. When you leave, you separate the dog from his "pack" and this creates separation anxiety. This behavior will be magnified if you tend to make a big fuss over the dog when leaving or returning to the house. Furthermore, certain other behavioral patterns on your part, such as rattling the car keys or turning off the television can be associated with your departure by the dog.

Treatment

When treating separation anxiety, one must remember that it is an instinctive behavior; it is not due to disobedience and/or lack or training.

Keep in Mind

Points to keep in mind when attempting to break your GSP of this annoying behavior are as follows:

1. Don't make a fuss over your dog within five to ten minutes of your arrival to or departure from home. This will help keep the excitement and anxiety levels in your dog to a minimum.
2. During your training sessions, try not to reenter the house while the dog is performing the undesirable act. Doing so will only serve to positively reinforce the dog to repeat the act.
3. Eliminate any behavior which may key the dog off to your departure, such as rattling your car keys, saying "goodbye" to your dog, etc.
4. For the dog that likes to chew a lot, provide plenty of nylon chew bones to occupy his time.
5. Leaving the television or radio on while you're gone seems to help in some cases.

As a result, punishment for the act tends to be unrewarding. In fact, most of these dogs would rather be punished than left alone. The key to treating this problem lies in planning short-term departures, then gradually lengthening them until your dog gets used to your absence. Begin by stepping out of the house for only a few seconds (10 to 15) at a time for the first few days or so. Hopefully this will allow your dog to get used to you leaving the house because he will learn that you will return soon. Vary your training session times throughout the day. The idea is to gradually lengthen your periods of absences (30 seconds at first, then one minute, then two minutes, etc.) so that your departures soon become second nature to the dog.

In severe cases, veterinarians can prescribe antianxiety medications such as clomipramine HCl (Clomicalm) to help assist in the treatment of separation anxiety. As a result, don't hesitate to contact your veterinarian if you are having difficulty solving your dog's separation anxiety problem.

Barking

Let's face it—some dogs just love to hear their own voice. Unfortunately, most owners and their neighbors hardly share the same admiration. There is no doubt that dogs that bark excessively are a nuisance and can cause many a sleepless night. For this reason, correcting the problem is essential to your sanity and those who live around you.

Causes

A dog may bark excessively for a number of reasons. The first is boredom. GSPs that have nothing else to do may simply "sing" to themselves to whittle away the time. Another potential cause is territoriality. Outsiders, human or animal, will almost always elicit a bark out of a dog if threatening to encroach upon its territory. Dogs may also use the bark indiscriminately as a communiqué to other outsiders to stay away. In such instances, the barking episode may be tipped off by the far-off bay of a neighborhood dog or the slamming of a car door down the street.

Separation anxiety is another common source of nuisance barking. Some dogs have it so bad that they bark continuously when their owner leaves them, even for a short period of time. Oftentimes, the owner will return home to find his dog hoarse from so much barking.

Breaking the Habit

When attempting to break your dog of this annoying habit, always remember this one principle: If you respond to your dog's barking by yelling at him or physically punishing him, you are going to make the problem worse. Dogs that are isolated from their owners for most of the day don't really care about what kind of attention they receive (positive or negative), just as long as they get some. Dogs that are barking out of boredom or from separation anxiety will soon learn that their action will eventually get

them attention, and they'll keep doing it. Even dogs that are barking for other reasons can catch on quickly that such vocalization will bring them a bonus of attention from their beloved owners. As a result, no matter how mad you get, or how sleepy you are, avoid the urge to punish your dog for his barking.

The first thing you need to determine is whether or not separation anxiety has anything to do with the problem. If you think it does, treat it as you would any other case of separation anxiety. In many cases, dogs that bark for this reason alone can be broken of their habit. Keep in mind, though, that the source of the barking may involve a combination of the factors, not just one.

GSPs that bark for other reasons besides separation anxiety need to be given more attention throughout the day. A dog that tends to bark through the night should be given plenty of exercise in the evening to encourage a good night's sleep. A nylon chew bone can be helpful at diverting his attention. Feeding his daily ration later in the evening may also promote contentment for the night.

For those times of the day or night that the barking seems the worst, consider bringing the dog inside the house or inside the garage. This, of course, may not be possible if you failed to instruct your dog as to the ways of household living when he was a puppy. Nevertheless, removing your dog from his "primary" territory and/or increasing the amount of contact with members of his pack can help curb his urge to bark. Also, if feasible, encourage your neighbors to keep their pets indoors at night because nighttime roaming activities of neighborhood dogs and cats are major causes of nuisance barking.

House Soiling

It has happened to all of us—the early morning encounter in the family room. The unexpected (or sometimes expected) surprise awaiting our arrival home from work. House soiling. It is a dirty habit, especially considering the size of the GSP. In many of these cases, the problem had an origin traceable to puppyhood; for others, it results from developmental behavioral and/or health problems. Regardless of the cause, you can take an active role in most cases to minimize or stop completely this annoying habit.

Common Causes

Lack of or improper house-training during puppyhood is undoubtedly the most common cause of house soiling. However, contrary to popular opinion, you *can* teach an old dog new tricks, but it just takes longer. With older canines that weren't properly house-trained, proceed with training or retraining as you would a puppy (see page 26). Along with lots of praise, a favorite treat or snack can also be used to reinforce desired behavior. For those times you can't be at home to monitor indoor activity, put him in a travel kennel or small bathroom because dogs are less likely to have premeditated accidents in such confined spaces. Just be reasonable as to the amount of time you make him wait between eliminations.

Inappropriate elimination activity can also result from separation anxiety. Dogs left on their own will often become frustrated and soil one or more parts of the house as a result. Some dogs will target furniture, bedding, and, if kept in the garage, even the roofs of automobiles. If the cause is truly separation anxiety, most of this adverse behavior will occur within 15 to 20 minutes after the owner departs; such predictability can assist in efforts to correct the problem. Treat as you would any other case of separation anxiety (see page 69).

The desire to delineate territory is another reason why a dog may choose to urinate (or sometimes defecate) indiscriminately. Certainly, intact male GSPs are more prone to this instinctive activity. Dogs have such a keen sense of smell that the mere presence of a canine trespasser around the perimeter of the home can set off a urine-marking binge. Owners who move into preowned homes often find out the hard way that the previous owners had a poorly trained or highly territorial house dog. Neutering your pet may or may not be helpful, depending upon his age. In many of these older males, it has become more habit than hormonal, and neutering does little to prevent it. Use of a pet odor neutralizer on the carpet and baseboards is warranted if you suspect that a previous occupant is to blame. Use of fencing or dog repellent (not poison) around the perimeter of the house may also help keep urine-markers away from your house.

An extremely submissive behavior often results in a cowering dog that urinates whenever anyone approaches. This type of adverse elimination is common in dogs that experienced adverse socialization as puppies or spent most of their growing years in a kennel or pound facility.

Management of Soiling Behavior

Management of such behavior focuses upon your actions and body language when approaching or greeting the dog.

✔ Try to avoid direct eye contact and sudden physical contact, for by doing so, you can send the dog into a submissive state.

✔ If you've been gone from the house for awhile, avoid sudden and exuberant greetings when you get home.

✔ By ignoring him initially, you'll lower your dog's excitement level, reduce the immediate threat to him, and give him no reason to urinate.

✔ One trick you can try right after you arrive is to casually walk over to your dog's food bowl and place some food or treats in it. The idea is to distract his attention away from the excitement of your arrival, and create a more comfortable, pleasing situation. Once you've been home awhile, then you can and should offer more of your attention.

Finally, be aware that some diseases or illnesses can cause a pet to urinate or defecate indiscriminately. For instance, dogs that tend to defecate inside the house should be checked for internal parasites. Diets increased in their fiber content can also increase the amount of trips your pet will need to take outdoors. Certainly, if the stools are semiformed, or seem to differ in normal appearance or consistency, an underlying medical reason should be suspected. Some of the conditions that can increase the frequency and/or urge to urinate include urinary tract infections, kidney disease, and diabetes mellitus. For this reason, don't just assume that your dog's soiling problem is purely mental. Have the potential medical causes ruled out first, then you can concentrate on behavior modification.

Cleaning Up Accidents

Just a word about cleaning up an accident in the house: When using cleaners to tackle the initial mess, be sure they don't contain ammonia. Dog urine contains a form of ammonia, and such products may actually attract your dog back to the same spot later on. Along this same line, after the initial manual cleaning, your next job is to ensure that residual smell doesn't attract your pet back to the same spot. To accomplish this, you need to employ a product containing odor neutralizers specifically targeted for dogs. These products are available in grocery stores or your favorite pet supply store. Deodorizers should not be used, for it is virtually impossible to completely mask or hide a scent from the keen canine nose.

Digging

Though separation anxiety can lead to digging, its influence is much less than with other problem behaviors. Instead, sheer boredom and/or instinctive behavior are the two common factors that compel a dog to dig. Dogs with nothing else to do may opt for yard excavation simply to help pass the time or use up extra energy. The urge to break out of confinement and roam the neighborhood can also compel a dog to start digging. Some dogs will dig to create a spot in which to lie and stay cool on a hot day. Finally, as you may have already experienced, many like to bury personal items such as bones or toys only for exhumation at a later date. Such instinctive behavior, though aggravating, can hardly be considered abnormal, and thus is difficult to totally eradicate.

Treatment

Increasing your dog's daily dose of exercise may be just what the doctor ordered to help resolve his boredom and release any pent-up energy. Diverting the attention of a chronic digger is another plausible treatment approach; for instance, some troublesome cases have responded very well to the addition of another canine playmate. Rawhide bones and other chewing devices can also be used as attention-grabbers, but only if they don't end up underground themselves. If most of the digging occurs at night, overnight confinement to the garage may be the answer to spare your yard from the ravages of claws. Finally, if not already done, neutering can sometimes help snuff out the strong urge to dig in those dogs wanting to roam the neighborhood.

Destructive Chewing

Many canines are literally "in the doghouse" with their owners because of this destructive behavior. No one wants a pet that seeks out and destroys any inanimate object he can sink his teeth into. However, the urgency for dealing with such behavior is not just governed by personal property damage. Many of these chewers also end up in veterinary hospitals suffering from gastroenteritis or intestinal obstructions. Hence, such adverse activity can cost more than just replacement value of furniture or fixtures; it can even sometimes cost the life of a pet.

In puppies, destructive chewing can easily arise from lack of training and from inappropriate selection of toys. Although puppies are naturally going to explore their environment with their mouths, they need to learn at an early age what is and isn't acceptable to chew on. Solid obedience training is a must in these little guys. Avoid providing normal household items such as old shoes, T-shirts, or sweatshirts as toys to play with. Puppies can't tell the difference between an old shoe and a new shoe, and may decide to try out your new pair for a snack one afternoon. Objects that repeatedly bear the brunt of your dog's teeth should obviously be placed as far out of reach as possible. For furniture or other immovable objects, special pet repellents should be sprayed around their perimeters to make a mischievous puppy think twice before sinking his teeth into the item.

In young to middle-aged GSPs, separation anxiety is probably the number one cause of destructive chewing. In these cases, the destructive behavior results from an owner's departure from the house, even for a few minutes. In these instances, correction of the problem should focus upon correction of the anxiety attack.

Finally, as with problem barking, boredom plays a leading role in destructive chewing in some adult dogs. If you think this may be the case, increase your dog's daily activity, and provide him with plenty of alternative targets, such

Monitor your puppy's chew toys.

as rawhides or nylon bones, on which to chew. Divert his attention, and most likely his chewing will be diverted as well.

Jumping

Talk about annoying behavior; this one is right up there with house soiling and incessant barking. "Jumpers," as we shall call them, are usually right there at the door when a visitor calls, and have this innate tendency to spoil a perfectly cordial greeting. After all, nobody wants a dog with dirty paws to jump on their nice, clean clothes, especially if the dog weighs 50 pounds (23 kg) or more.

This is one problem behavior that should never be allowed to gain a firm foothold in a puppy. Probably the best way to assure this is through strict obedience training, starting at an early age. Until he learns his commands, discourage him from jumping on you or family members when the occasion arises. When he does jump at or on you, flex your knee and make sudden but gentle contact with his chest, making him fall backward. Then ignore your dog as if nothing happened.

Note: For adult dogs that never learned their manners, a refresher course in obedience training is the most effective method of curing the chronic jumper. Sometimes, dogs that jump may be simply trying to tell their owners that they want more attention. In such cases, a few more moments of your time devoted to your GSP each day is an important adjunct to therapy.

Fear of Loud Noises

Fear induced by loud noises such as thunder or fireworks can be a cause of aberrant behavior in GSPs. Many persons may argue that because of the ultra-sensitive hearing of dogs, pain and pressure changes induced by noise may play a bigger role than fear of the strange noise itself. Regardless of the reason, when confronted with the disturbing sound, these dogs often become hysterical and quite destructive in their attempts to escape. Many may injure themselves or their owners in the process.

Treatment

For dogs that fear the sound of thunder, fireworks, etc., owners must avoid direct attempts at comforting the pet; doing so would be indirectly rewarding the undesirable behavior. If your dog is the type that comes unglued in these situations, consider letting him "ride out the storm" in his travel kennel. In addition, playing a radio or television loudly in the vicinity of your pet may help muffle some of the fearful sounds, as well as make your GSP feel more at ease. Your veterinarian can prescribe antianxiety medications for your dog if he has an exceptional fear of these types of loud noises. In any event, these medications should be used sparingly and only as needed.

Aggressiveness

Of all the undesirable behaviors a dog may exhibit, this one is certainly the most disturbing and the most unacceptable. The aggressiveness may be directed toward other dogs, or toward other species, including humans. Certainly, dogs harboring an uncontrollable inherent aggressiveness toward the latter pose special problems

to their owners in terms of liability as well. Fortunately, aggressiveness is rarely a problem in the GSP.

Dominance

Dominance certainly plays an important role in canine aggressiveness. Some dogs refuse to submit to authority and will lash out at anyone or anything that attempts to exert the authority. In many instances, these dogs were not properly socialized and/or trained when they were young. In others, sex hormones, namely testosterone, may exert a strong influence as well.

Treatment

Treatment for such aggressiveness consists of a return to basic obedience training. In addition, exercises designed to reestablish dominance can be recommended by your veterinarian and should be performed as well. If the aggression is directed toward a particular person in general, that person too should be included in these exercises. Extreme caution and a good, strong muzzle are both advised before any attempts at such dominance assertion are made. For domineering male dogs, neutering is recommended prior to any attempts at retraining.

Fear and Pain

Fear and pain are two other common causes of aggressiveness in canines. If a dog feels threatened or overwhelmingly fearful, it naturally experiences a "fight or flight" syndrome and may choose the former option over the latter, depending upon how he perceives his options. In addition, dogs have been known to naturally lash out in fear at humans or other animals upon being startled, or more frequently, when experiencing pain. For this reason, sudden aggressive changes in personality with or without other signs of illness warrant a complete checkup by your veterinarian.

Treatment

Treating fear-induced aggression is aimed at reducing the threat you or others pose to your pet. If fear aggression is induced by some outside stimulus, such as a gunshot, then proper restraint and isolation is recommended while the stimulus lasts. If a dog suffers from a vision or hearing deficit, attempts should be made to capture the dog's attention prior to approach.

Note: Not only is physical punishment a useless tool for training, it can lead to natural, aggressive backlashes due to pain (and fear). This is just one more reason why such punishment should be avoided.

Injuries and Illnesses

For those dogs suffering from injuries or illnesses, approach and handle them with caution, for although they may not mean to, they could exhibit aggressive tendencies due to the pain associated with the disease.

Territoriality

Dogs, male or female, will certainly defend that property they deem theirs, and may not hesitate to fight for it. Territorial aggressiveness toward unwelcome animals or people is not uncommon, as any utilities meter reader would attest to. Such aggressive behavior can be just as easily sparked by a perceived encroachment while the dog is eating, or while it is playing with its favorite toy. Many bite wounds to owners have been inflicted because of such actions.

Treatment

A return to the basics of obedience training with or without neutering should help curb some of the territorial aggressiveness that may be exhibited by some dogs. In those instances where dogs exhibit aggressiveness toward other dogs they deem a threat to their territory, neutering will usually help in the majority of the cases.

Certainly showing some respect for a dog's "private property" (toys, bowls, etc.) and eating privacy is a commonsense way to avoid this type of aggressive behavior. It is of vital importance to impress this concept upon children because they can be frequent violators of the rule. If a dog seems particularly possessive over toys, bones, and so on, then excessive sources of the problem should be reduced by eliminating all but one or two of the items. Also, consider feeding the dog in an isolated area of the house away from disturbances.

The best treatment for most types of aggression is prevention. By adhering to the principles of proper socialization and by proper obedience training, most behavioral problems related to aggressiveness can be avoided altogether. However, for any GSP exhibiting aggressiveness, a thorough physical examination and consultation with a veterinarian is indicated. Ruling out underlying medical causes is certainly one reason for this; the other is that your veterinarian may choose to prescribe medications to assist in retraining efforts or as a direct attempt to curb the psychological aspects of your dog's aggressiveness. Ask your pet's doctor for more details.

TRAVELING WITH YOUR GERMAN SHORTHAIRED POINTER

As a rule, GSPs make good travel companions. Rarely do they become frantic or sick to their stomachs when placed inside a moving object. However, whenever you plan on traveling with your GSP, whether on an extended vacation or a short trip to the local grocery store, there are some guidelines that you should follow to ensure a safe, pleasant experience for you and your pet.

Traveling by Car

When traveling with your GSP by automobile, always keep the safety and comfort of both driver and passenger in mind. A dog allowed to roam freely in the front seat of a car poses a serious driving hazard. In addition, your vehicle's airbags can easily kill a dog if they deploy. As a result, always have your pet restrained in the back seat of your car, not the front. Better yet, if one will fit into your car or truck, use a travel carrier to transport your GSP.

When traveling by car, your GSP should be properly restrained.

Keep the interior of your car cool and well-ventilated. GSPs that are excited and forced to travel in hot stuffy cars or those filled with cigarette smoke can hyperventilate and overheat. Also, car exhaust fumes can quickly overcome a GSP left inside an idling car. If you become stuck in traffic, be sure to crack the windows and keep the air circulating within the car. And never leave a dog unattended in a parked car if outside temperatures exceed 72°F (22°C) or drop below 55°F (13°C). If you do, your dog could succumb to heatstroke or hypothermia.

If your car ride is going to last for more than an hour, be sure you take along plenty of

ture and/or pressure fluctuations occur during flight, they could be harmful to a GSP suffering from an underlying heart condition.

Temperature Extremes

Because your dog will travel cargo, book either an early evening or early morning flight during the summer months and midday flights during winter months to protect from temperature extremes. Also, book direct flights only so that there's no chance of "lost baggage." If possible, plan on arriving early enough at the gate so that you can observe your pet being loaded onto the plane.

Carriers to Rent

If you own a pet carrier that is not fit for air travel, most airlines have carriers for rent; however, be sure that the pet carrier selected for your pet is the proper size for his safety during the flight. Call ahead of time to confirm carrier availability.

You will want to pad the inside of the carrier liberally with large blankets and/or towels. And don't forget to throw in one of your pet's favorite toys. A "Live Animal" sticker, as well as your name, address, and phone number, should be attached conspicuously to the outside of the carrier.

Avoid feeding your GSP solid food within six hours of the plane trip. Provide a constant source of water during the flight by freezing water in a water bowl the night prior to your trip and placing this in your pet's carrier prior to the flight.

water for your GSP to drink and plan on making frequent potty stops along the way. Ice makes an excellent, spill-free source of water for these long trips.

If your GSP tends to get sick when traveling in a car, talk to your veterinarian, who can recommend several over-the-counter remedies than prevent carsickness in dogs.

Taking to the Skies

If you are planning to transport your GSP by plane, consult your veterinarian prior to your trip to determine whether or not your pet has any medical conditions that may prohibit such travel, for example, should significant tempera-

Vacation Planning

Prior to leaving on your vacation, make certain you are aware of all the requirements necessary for taking your GSP to his intended destination, including health certificates, local quarantines, and customs. When traveling domestically and interstate with your pet, two items you should always have with you are your pet's vaccination record and a current health certificate. A licensed veterinarian must issue this health certificate within 10 days of your trip. If traveling overseas, the embassy of the country of destination can inform you of all of the necessary requirements for the safe and legal transport of your pet.

Motels, Hotels, Campgrounds

Consult travel guides or travel agents to find listings of those motels, hotels, and campgrounds that accept pets and plan your overnight stops around these locations. When you arrive at your destination, look in the local phone directory for the name and number of a local veterinarian in the area, just in case of emergency.

Try not to leave your GSP unattended in your motel or hotel room. If you do, be sure to place the "Do Not Disturb" sign on the front door so that your pet doesn't accidentally escape if housekeeping comes to clean your room while you are away.

When camping with your pet, don't allow him to roam or to interact with wild animals; being natural hunters, GSPs will quickly get themselves in trouble. It's also a great idea to have your GSP checked out by your veterinarian following these camping trips to be sure he didn't pick up any unwanted parasites from the local fauna.

Boarding

Finally, there will be times when your GSP will be better off at home versus traveling with

TIP

Travel Advice

✔ Be sure the carrier you have for your dog is sturdy and in good condition.

✔ Also, make sure your pet's collar has identification tags, including a phone number, if possible, of where you'll be staying just in case your pet gets lost.

✔ You'll want to take a leash along for daily exercise, as well as your GSP's brush for daily grooming.

✔ Finally, plan on taking plenty of your dog's food along with you, just in case the brand you normally feed your GSP is not available at your destination.

you. In these instances, choose a kennel facility for your dog as you would a hotel for yourself, making sure it is clean, well ventilated, and staffed by caring people. Many newer facilities are equipped with interactive cameras attached to each run or pen that can be accessed over the Internet, allowing you to check in on your pet even if you happen to be on the other side of the world. Although it costs more to board a pet at such a facility, many owners feel that it is well worth the price.

Pet Sitters

Another great alternative is to keep your GSP at home and hire a pet sitter to check in on your pet throughout the day. If you can't find a neighbor or friend to oblige, check your phone book for a professional pet sitter near you, or ask your veterinarian for a referral.

THE THRILL OF COMPETITION

If you long for the thrill of competition, consider entering your GSP in one of the many AKC or FDSB (Field Dog Stud Book) licensed events occurring throughout the county. Competitive events held under American Kennel Club rules include conformation dog shows, companion events, and performance events.

Events

Conformation shows judge dogs on how closely they match the breed conformational and physical standards as established by their respective national breed clubs (visit *www.akc.org* for the Official Breed Standard for the GSP). Next, companion events include obedience trials, tracking tests, dog agility events, AKC Rally events, and Junior Showmanship competitions. Finally, performance events for GSPs include field trials and hunting tests.

Before entering your dog into any event, make plans to attend several trials as a spectator in order to gain a better understanding of that particular event's procedures and rules. Make the most of your time by mingling with fellow spectators and contestants, asking questions

A GSP competing in an agility event.

liberally. In fact, it is a good idea to write your questions down prior to attending the event to be sure you come away with a full database. Also, ask for recommendations pertaining to any books, literature, publications, Internet addresses, electronic mailboxes, podcasts, and/or chat rooms that could serve to further enhance your knowledge on the subject. Obviously, the more information you can amass prior to your dog becoming an actual contestant, the better are the chances for success for you and your dog when your time comes to compete.

Locations of events in your area can be traced through your local breeders, veterinarians, trainers, dog clubs, and hunt clubs. You can also contact the AKC and FDSB directly for listings of competitions in your locale. A wealth of information can also be searched and retrieved via the Internet concerning competitions for your GSP (see Appendix, page 92).

Breed Standard

For the Official Breed Standard of the German Shorthaired Pointer, visit the American Kennel Club's web site.

The GSP should possess a conformation of symmetry and balance, with a well-muscled appearance that reflects the breed's strength and fortitude. Movements reflect grace and purpose, and should show no signs of awkwardness. Mental alertness, combined with enthusiasm and intelligence, are expected in ideal representatives of the breed.

Size and Color

Adult males should stand 23 to 25 inches (58–63.5 cm) at the withers, whereas females should be 21 to 23 inches (53–58 cm). Deviations of more than 1 inch (2.5 cm) either way are penalized. As far as weight is concerned, males should tip the scales anywhere from 55 to 70 pounds (25–32 cm), whereas females should weigh no less than 45 pounds (20 kg) and no more than 60 pounds (27 kg). The tail should be docked in such a way as to leave 40 percent of its original length; any more or any less threatens to disrupt body symmetry. Dewclaws on the forelegs may be removed without fault.

Acceptable coat color patterns include solid liver or any combination of liver and white. Aberrant colors, such as black, red, orange, lemon, or tan, that appear anywhere on the coat, are grounds for disqualification. A solid white hair coat will be disqualified as well.

Faults: Faults include any and all physical and/or mental deviations that interfere with the intended function of the breed. Barrel chests, excessive forehead wrinkles, pointed or dish-faced muzzles, curved or bent tails, spotted nares, long or sway backs, excessively large ear-flaps, stilted or abrupt gaits caused by abnormal joint alignments, aggressiveness, and/or timidity are just some examples of undesirable traits. In addition to the aberrant coat colors mentioned previously, disqualifying features include china or wall eyes, flesh-colored nares, and overshot or undershot jaws.

Shows and Tests

Conformation Shows

There are three types of conformation shows sanctioned by the AKC. These include All-breed Shows, Specialty Shows, and Group Shows. As the name implies, all-breed shows are competitions in which different AKC breeds compete with one another in the same venues (interbreed competitions). In contrast, specialty shows restrict competitions to specific breeds only (intrabreed competitions). Group shows limit participation to those individuals belonging to a particular AKC-recognized dog group (Sporting, Hound, Working, Terrier, Toy, Non-Sporting, and Herding). In other words, the GSP, which is a member of the Sporting Group, cannot compete in a group show designed for working breeds. Different types of conformation shows are often held in conjunction with one another under one roof. Judging is based on the process of elimination, with the overall winner being crowned "Best in Show."

In order for your GSP to compete in conformation shows, he must be registered with the AKC and meet eligibility standards for the breed. He also must be at least six months of age, intact (not spayed or castrated), and eligible for the breed class offered at a particular show. For information on how conformation

dog shows are classed and scored, as well as tips and articles on how to prepare and get involved in these events, visit the AKC web site.

Obedience Trials

In obedience trials, dogs are led through a series of exercises and commands, with judges scoring their performances along the way. There are multiple levels or titles that dogs compete for in obedience trials, with the ultimate goal of becoming "Obedience Trial Champion." Each dog-handler team starts out with a set number of points, and then points are deducted for slowness, lack of attention, and/or vocalization.

In fact, if a handler must repeat a command, the team is automatically disqualified.

Unlike dog shows, scoring for obedience trials has nothing to do with physical conformation. In fact, dogs that have been neutered or have other physical defects are still welcome to compete in these events. However, all four-legged contestants must be at least six months of age to enter.

Tracking Tests

Tracking tests are also exciting competitive events for GSPs. These competitions are designed to measure the nasal qualities of the individual competitors; that is, their ability to follow a scent that has been aged over a specified distance. A dog can accumulate points and titles from these events that can eventually earn it the coveted title of "Champion Tracker."

Agility Events

In agility competitions, dogs are guided by their owners over a course filled with obstacles they must jump over, tires and tunnels they must go through, and poles they must weave in and out of. These are timed events, measuring agility under pressure. Penalties are assessed if obstacles are missed or knocked down, or if time runs out before the course is finished. As with other types of competitive events, various levels of proficiency receive awards, from the most basic to the most advanced agility talents.

Rally Events

In rally events, canine contestants are run through courses that test their obedience and agility talents. Unlike obedience trials, handlers are allowed to use hand gestures, generous voice commands, and exaggerated body language to urge their dogs through the course, and the judging is not as rigorous as in regular obedience events. The AKC Rally is an excellent way for Canine Good Citizens to prepare for the more challenging AKC obedience and agility competitions.

Junior Showmanship

Designed for individuals under 18 years of age, junior showmanship conformation events give young dog owners a "taste" of what conformation dog shows are all about by judging their abilities to present and handle their dogs within similar formats and guidelines as the adult conformation shows. Young contestants are judged on handling abilities, personal appearance, dog grooming, and conduct within the ring. As members of the AKC Junior Organization, young men and women can also compete in companion and performance events with their pets, earning special recognition, awards, and, most importantly, invaluable experience for the future.

Good Citizen Test

The Good Citizen Test evaluates a dog's ability and willingness to behave and act properly in public, reflecting the handler's own aptitude as a trainer. As a matter of interest, this is the only AKC-sponsored activity that allows mixed-breed dogs to participate. Ten different tests are administered, all on a pass-fail basis. They include the following:

• **Test 1:** Accepting a friendly stranger. Your dog must show no signs of aggression, shyness, or jealousy when approached by the evaluator. He must not break his position or jump on the evaluator.

• **Test 2:** Sitting politely for petting (by a friendly stranger). Your dog must sit and not move when approached and petted by the evaluator.

• **Test 3:** Appearance and grooming. Your dog should allow grooming and hands-on examination by the evaluator. He is allowed to move during the actions, but should not struggle.

• **Test 4:** Out for a walk/walking on loose leash. In this test, your pet should maneuver on a leash without pulling, struggling, or disobeying commands.

• **Test 5:** Walking through a crowd. This examines your dog's ability to stay under control when walking in a public place with other people around.

- **Test 6:** Sitting and lying down on command and staying in place. As far as the latter is concerned, your dog must remain in place until the evaluator instructs you to release him.
- **Test 7:** Coming when called. As the name implies, this test determines if your dog will indeed come when called.
- **Test 8:** Reaction to other dogs. This is a test to see how your dog reacts around his peers. Grading will depend on your pet's ability to remain calm and in control when other dogs are brought around.
- **Test 9:** Reaction to distractions. Your dog must not be easily distracted by passing bicycles, joggers, or by sudden noises.
- **Test 10:** Supervised separation. Can your dog be left alone with the stranger without becoming distraught? This test will tell.

If you and your dog pass all ten tests, you are then allowed to apply for the coveted Canine Good Citizen certificate and special collar tag for your well-mannered GSP.

Field Trials

For the serious enthusiast, field trials offer a chance to extend the thrill of the hunt beyond bird season. They also provide an excellent venue for honing hunting skills and maintaining a bird dog in top condition. Field trials are designed to test the ability of a dog to perform the original functions of the breed of which it is a member. GSPs compete in field trials designated for the pointing breeds. These trials include exercises that test the ability of the dog to scent out game, to go on point, and to remain staunch on that point.

Over 1,000 of these competitive events are held throughout the United States each year. Most are conducted on weekends, held by clubs operating under either AKC or FDSB rules. A single field trial actually consists of a number of competitions, or stakes. Individual stakes are characterized by certain restrictions and rules designed to maintain a competitive fairness. Qualifications for individual stakes take into account the experience of the handler, the method of transportation used in the stake (such as horseback versus walking on foot), the age of the dog, and the dog's past accomplishments. Each dog and/or handler is allowed to enter all stakes for which the imposed restrictions are met.

Various courses are designed to simulate natural hunting conditions and scenarios. Competing dogs hunt planted game such as quail and pheasant. During each stake, dogs are run in pairs (braces), with the handlers following behind on horseback or on foot. The judges and trial marshal generally follow all of the action on horseback.

Hunting Tests

Hunting tests are noncompetitive sporting events sanctioned by the American Kennel Club. For the pointing breeds, these tests first appeared back in 1986. Most are organized and run by AKC field trial clubs or by individual breed clubs. Whereas field trials are highly competitive events that match dog against dog for the title of "top dog," hunting tests are more laid back, with participants competing against established hunting standards rather than against other participants. The result: A recreational and relaxed event in which there is no pressure to beat the competition. Hunting tests are fun and ideal for the hobbyist who enjoys interacting with fellow bird dog owners.

YOUR DOG'S GOLDEN YEARS

Genetics, nutrition, and environmental influences all ultimately affect the aging process differently in each particular individual.

As a rule, GSPs should be considered "geriatric" once they reach their seventh year (the breed's average lifespan is around 12 years). However, just because your dog has reached a particular benchmark in years doesn't mean that the aging changes that are occurring within his body necessarily reflect those years.

It is a fact that the overall care a dog receives throughout his life will also have a great impact upon the rate of aging. GSPs that have been well cared for throughout puppyhood and adult life tend to suffer fewer infirmities as they grow old than do less fortunate canine counterparts. By practicing diligent preventive health care, the impact of many age-related health problems can be diminished.

As your dog gets older, special care will be required.

Mental and Physical Changes

As your GSP matures, it will undergo mental and physical changes resulting from years of wear and tear on all body systems.

✔ To begin, a reduction in the overall metabolic rate usually occurs, leading to reduced activity and a predisposition to weight gain.

✔ The heart becomes less efficient at pumping blood, causing an earlier onset of fatigue during exercise and hunting activities.

✔ Joint pain and reduced joint mobility may arise due to arthritis.

✔ A general atrophy of the muscles of limbs and hips occurs due to decreased muscle activity and due to age-related protein loss from the body.

✔ As your GSP grows older, he may also experience skin and coat problems resulting from aging effects upon the hair cycle and from metabolic and endocrine upsets.

✔ The kidneys become less efficient at filtering wastes.

✔ A decrease in liver function makes it more difficult to metabolize nutrients and detoxify poisons within the body.

✔ Fertility and reproductive performance diminish, and the incidence of uterine, mammary, and/or prostate disease increases, especially in non-neutered dogs.

✔ The gastrointestinal tract exhibits a reduced tolerance to dietary fluctuations and excesses.

✔ The ability to digest food properly may become partially impaired, predisposing to flare-ups of gastritis, colitis, and constipation.

✔ It is well-documented that the efficiency and activity of the immune system also become compromised with age. As a result, geriatric pets are more susceptible to disease, especially viruses and cancer.

✔ In addition, the activity of the endocrine glands within the body may start to diminish, leaving your pet with hormone-related challenges such as hypothyroidism and diabetes mellitus.

✔ As one might expect, the aging process adversely affects mental acuity as well, which may result in noticeable senile behavior.

Senses

Finally, your dog's senses are no less susceptible to Father Time. For starters, older GSPs may develop a slight grayish white or bluish haze to the lenses of both eyes, termed nuclear sclerosis, or they may develop actual cataracts, the latter leading to much greater visual impairment. In addition to reduced eyesight, partial or total hearing loss is common in geriatric GSPs,

especially those that have been exposed to gunfire for much of their lives. It is the sense of smell that is usually the last to go in older dogs. As a result, old-timers come to depend more and more on their sense of smell (rather than sight or sound) to identify people, objects, and food. Obviously, challenges in these areas can occur as this sense begins to fail. A reduced sense of smell, combined with taste buds that don't work quite as well as they used to, can lead to finicky eating behaviors and/or reduced appetites in senior adults.

As mentioned previously, the speed at which the above changes occur will vary greatly between individual dogs, and will be affected by genetics, environment, nutrition, and by the amount of preventive health care provided. Keeping these in mind, here are a few items to note as your dog grows older:

✔ Adjust your GSP's diet to match his specific health needs. For example, if your dog suffers from an age-related ailment such as heart disease or colitis, special diets may be prescribed to reduce the wear and tear on the affected organ systems. For the otherwise healthy seniors, feed a diet that is higher in fiber and reduced in calories to prevent obesity.

✔ Weigh your dog on a monthly basis. Persistent weight loss or weight gain should be reported to your veterinarian.

✔ Maintain a moderate exercise program for your older dog, especially during the hunting off-season. This will help keep his bones, joints, heart, and lungs conditioned. Always consult your veterinarian first as to the type and amount of exercise appropriate for your older pet.

✔ Groom and brush your dog daily. Skin and coat changes secondary to aging, such as oily skin and abnormal shedding, can often be man-

A sound preventive health care program can keep your GSP fit and active well into his senior years.

aged well with proper grooming. In addition, keep those toenails trimmed short. Older dogs suffering from arthritis don't need the added challenge and pain of having to ambulate with nails growing to the floor.

✔ Semiannual veterinary checkups, routine teeth cleaning, and periodic at-home physical examinations for aging pets are a must. Remember: Early detection of a disease is the key to curing or managing the disorder. Also, because of the effects aging has on the immune system, keep your dog current on his vaccinations.

✔ Be considerate of your older dog's limitations both mentally and physically. Keep food and water bowls easily accessible. Provide ramps where necessary to help the arthritic dog negotiate steps and heights. To compensate for decreased sensory awareness, approach older dogs slower than you would younger ones, using a calm, reassuring voice to further enhance recognition.

✔ Finally, give your old friend plenty of quality attention each day, continually reinforcing the companionship and bond that you two share together.

By following these tips, you can do your part to ensure that your GSP grows old gracefully and experiences golden years that are filled with health and happiness.

Registries

American Kennel Club (AKC)
5580 Centerview Drive
Raleigh, NC 27606-3390
www.akc.org

Field Dog Stud Book (FDSB)
542 South Dearborn Street
Chicago, IL 60605
www.americanfield.com

United Kennel Club (UKC)
100 East Kilgore Road
Kalamazoo, MI 49001-5598
www.ukcdogs.com

Field Trial/Hunting Clubs and Associations

Amateur Field Trial Clubs of America
   (AFTCA)
1300 Tripp Road
Somerville, TN 38068
www.aftca.org

American Bird Hunters Association (ABHA)
www.abhatrials.com

North American Versatile Hunting Dog
   Association (NAVHDA)
P.O. Box 520
Arlington Heights, IL 60006
www.navhda.org

National Bird Hunters Association (NBHA)
P.O. Box 68
Winfield, AL 35594
www.nbhafuturity.com

National Shoot-to-Retrieve Association (NSTRA)
226 North Mill Street #2
Plainfield, IN 46168
www.nstra.org

Breed Clubs

German Shorthaired Pointer Club of America
www.gspca.org

National German Shorthaired Pointer
   Association
P.O. Box 12263
Overland Park, KS 66212
www.ngspa.org

Other Organizations

The Bird Dog Foundation, Inc.
P.O. Box 774
Grand Junction, TN 38039
www.birddogfoundation.com

German Shorthaired Pointer Rescue
www.gsprescue.org

Magazines and Periodicals

The American Field
542 South Dearborn Street
Chicago, IL 60605
www.americanfield.com

Gun Dog Magazine
P.O. Box 420234
Palm Coast, FL 32142-0234
www.gundogmag.com

*Hunting Test Herald/ Pointing Breed
   Field Trial News*
51 Madison Avenue
New York, NY 10010

The Pointing Dog Journal
2779 Aero Park Drive
Traverse City, MI 49686
www.pointingdogjournal.com

Wing & Shot
P.O. Box 343
Mt. Morris, IL 61054

Dog Fancy Magazine
P.O. Box 53264
Boulder, CO 80322-3264

AKC Gazette
51 Madison Avenue
New York, NY 10010

Consult organization web sites for any updates
regarding contact information

Useful Web Sites

American Kennel Club (AKC)
www.akc.org

American Veterinary Medical Association
www.avma.org

Dog Fancy Magazine
www.dogfancy.com

Field Dog Stud Book (FDSB)
www.americanfield.com

United Kennel Club (UKC)
www.ukcdogs.com

Amateur Field Trial Clubs of America (AFTCA)
www.aftca.org

American Bird Hunters Association (ABHA)
www.abhatrials.com

North American Versatile Hunting Dog
   Association (NAVHDA)
www.navhda.org

National Bird Hunters Association (NBHA)
www.nbhafuturity.com

National Shoot-to-Retrieve Association (NSTRA)
www.nstra.org

German Shorthaired Pointer Club of America
www.gspca.org

National German Shorthaired Pointer Association
www.ngspa.org

The Bird Dog Foundation, Inc.
www.birddogfoundation.com

German Shorthaired Pointer Rescue
www.gsprescue.org

The American Field
www.americanfield.com

Gun Dog Magazine
www.gundogmag.com

The Pointing Dog Journal
www.pointingdogjournal.com

Training Books

Healy, Joe. *Training a Young Pointer*. Stackpole
   Books, 2005.
Smith, Jason. *Dog Training: Retrievers and
   Pointing Dogs (The Complete Hunter)*.
   Creative Publishing International, 2007.

About the Author

Chris C. Pinney, DVM is a practicing veterinarian from Schulenburg, Texas. He has authored six books pertaining to pets, including *Guide to Home Pet Grooming*, *Caring for Your Older Dog*, and the award-winning *Caring for Your Older Cat*, by Barron's Educational Series, Inc.

Photo Credits

Kent Akselsen: pages 16, 19, 28, 36, 47, 48, 49, 57, 59, 60, 78; Norvia Behling: pages 5, 9, 10, 12, 20, 24, 45, 69, 75, 83; Kent Dannen: pages 2, 3, 4, 17, 21, 29, 30, 34, 50, 65, 67, 68, 71, 80, 85, 89; Cheryl Ertelt: pages 14, 56, 61, 66, 82, 88, 91; Jean M. Fogle: 13, 15, 25, 37, 79; Isabelle Francais: pages 8, 22, 23, 41, 46, 55, 62; Connie Summers: page 54

Cover Credits

Front and back covers: Shutterstock; inside front and inside back covers: Jean M. Fogle

All inquiries should be addressed to:
Barron's Educational Series, Inc.
250 Wireless Boulevard
Hauppauge, NY 11788
www.barronseduc.com

ISBN-13: 978-0-7641-3770-9
ISBN-10: 0-7641-3770-0

Library of Congress Catalog Card No. 2007028723

Library of Congress Cataloging-in-Publication Data
Pinney, Chris C.
    German shorthaired pointers : everything about purchase, care, nutrition, behavior, and training / Chris C. Pinney.
        p. cm.
    Includes index.
    ISBN-13: 978-0-7641-3770-9
    ISBN-10: 0-7641-3770-0
    1. German shorthaired pointer. I. Title.

SF429.G4P55   2008
636.752′5—dc22   2007028723

Printed in China
9 8 7 6 5 4 3 2 1

Important Note

Always use caution and common sense whenever handling a dog, especially one that may be ill or injured. Employ proper restraint devices as necessary. In addition, if the information and procedures contained in this book differ in any way from your veterinarian's recommendations concerning your pet's health care, please consult him/her prior to their implementation. Finally, because each pet is unique, always consult your veterinarian before administering any type of treatment or medication to your pet.